D1611751

SITTING IN

HAYDEN CARRUTH

SELECTED WRITINGS
ON JAZZ, BLUES, AND
RELATED TOPICS

SITTING IN

UNIVERSITY OF IOWA PRESS

IOWA CITY

University of Iowa Press, Iowa City 52242

Copyright © 1986 by the University of Iowa

Printed in the United States of America

First edition, 1986

Book and jacket design by Richard Hendel

Typesetting by G & S Typesetters, Inc., Austin, Texas

Printing and binding by Edwards Brothers, Inc., Ann Arbor, Michigan

Library of Congress Cataloging-in-Publication Data

Carruth, Hayden, 1921–

Sitting in.

1. Afro-Americans—Music—Collected works.
2. Jazz music—Collected works.   3. Blues (Songs, etc.)
—Collected works.   I. Title.
ML3556.C37   1986   781'.57   86-7042
ISBN 0-87745-153-2

Dedicated to
Brad Morrow and Hank O'Neal

CONTENTS

ACKNOWLEDGMENTS

Some pieces in this book were first published in the following magazines, to whose publishers and editors I am grateful: *Conjunctions, American Book Review, Ironwood, The Hudson Review, Poetry East, The Georgia Review, The Sewanee Review, The Kenyon Review,* and *The CEA Critic.* A few are reprinted from earlier books, which are still in print: *Brothers, I Loved You All* (Sheep Meadow Press, 1978), *If You Call This Cry a Song* (Countryman Press, 1983), *Effluences from the Sacred Caves* (University of Michigan Press, 1983), *The Oldest Killed Lake in North America* (Salt-Works Press, 1985), *Lighter Than Air Craft* (Press of Appletree Alley, 1985), and *The Selected Poetry of Hayden Carruth* (Macmillan, 1986).

PREFACE

Although the earliest piece in this book was written in 1948, by far the greater number have been done in the past three or four years, and their arrangement here is thematic, in loose clusters of thought and feeling, rather than chronological. The focus is on jazz. A few literary pieces, however, written during the same time as most of the jazz pieces and reflecting similar concerns, are included as well.

I have tried to eliminate repetition from the essays, but because they were written on varied occasions, some unavoidable repetition remains. So does a certain amount of opinion, which I myself distrust, as in my pessimistic remarks about young writers and the tendencies of the present age. But one must rest somewhere. To offer contrary opinion and countervailing evidence in every case would seem unlikely to readers and unbearably discouraging to myself.

Jazz and poetry have been closely interrelated in my life for fifty years. It was not my aim in these essays, poems, and reviews to demonstrate a similar relationship in the life of the nation, yet when the pieces are taken together, they do appear to be moving in that direction. Who would wish to disguise it? The Afroamerican components of our civilization, not just the music and other arts but many far more pervasive elements of attitude and sensibility, seem to me obvious, necessary, edifying, and largely determinative. Hence the black part of our consciousness—our thought, vision, speech, feeling, sensual responsiveness, our whole being—is what I would celebrate. Some people will think this at variance with the Yankee proclivity of my other poems or the broadly historical and European orientation of my other essays, but perhaps this book will prove that these apparent incompatibilities are apparent only.

To all who have helped me toward whatever understanding I possess of jazz and poetry, my thanks. Some are named in this book, but inevitably most are not. What is more important is the paradox, which nevertheless is my conviction, that those who are devoted primarily to jazz, to poetry, to all the arts, are also those who contribute more intelligently than others to our practical and moral, political and social, advancement. Jazz is love. Poetry is peace.

—*H.C.*

SITTING IN

THE GUY DOWNSTAIRS

Once forty-odd years ago I read an account by someone, I don't re-member who, of a visit with Jack Teagarden in the room of a third-rate hotel in Manhattan. That must have been in the early 1930s. A good many musicians were living in third-rate hotels in those days, and were lucky if they could afford the rent at that. The room was shabby, small, and sparely furnished. Big T, as he was called, lay on an iron bedstead, and within arm's reach he had a record player on the floor and a scattering of records. Was it an electric player? I don't know; I believe there were portable spring-driven players (Victrolas) in those days with cranks small enough so that the handle could be turned when the machine was resting on the floor. The main thing I recall from the account of the visit was how Teagarden from time to time sprawled his big frame side-ways on the bed and put an Armstrong record on the turntable and played it, listening intently. Each time, when the record ended, he said something like: "Hear that, man. Hear that."

That was all. And for anyone who didn't have a tin ear, it was enough.

Yet I find myself now writing more and more about jazz, both in poetry and in prose, partly, no doubt, because in old age one no longer minds revealing one's sources, but partly also because I see very clearly now how important jazz has been not only to my own writing but, directly or indirectly, to almost everyone's.

At a later time, when I lived in Chicago (1946–52), I became friends with Don Ewell, who played piano with Big T several years later in the fifties, both in the big bands and in smaller groups. (He can be heard on Teagarden's records from those years, includ-ing taped concerts from Okinawa and other locations on the tour-ing itinerary.) Don was not a great musician, but he might have been. What I mean is that he was driven into professional per-forming by his irresistible love of jazz, but his personality was not suited to playing in public or, even worse, into a microphone. I've rarely heard him when he was really on in public, and none of his records—there are quite a few—represents him at his best, as far as I know. Don grew up in a small town in Delaware in the 1920s, and first heard jazz on records, perhaps on the radio. Much later he studied for a year or two at the conservatory in Baltimore (where Sidney Lanier had played and taught). He became an eastern, stride piano player here and there before the war, did his hitch in an army band during the war (played triangle if I remember correctly), then linked up with Bunk Johnson after he was discharged. When I first met him, Don had recently been released from the laughing academy, as he called it, and had two considerable scars on his wrists. He was anxious and tense. He had a nervous little laugh that was always cut off abruptly, his face stiffening into shy blankness, as if he had caught himself in a *gaucherie.* When he sat at the piano, however, he was ok, more or less, and had a certain authority, almost unobservable to anyone who didn't know him, in his posture and movements. He was drinking and taking bennies and greenies, but not too much. In fact he was in pretty good shape. He gigged around Chicago and nearby towns, but mostly at Jazz, Ltd., on the Near North and at the Bee Hive on 55th Street, as sleazy a neighborhood of rough bars, after-hours clubs, policy joints, etc., as you would care to see.

I was with Don the night we heard of Bunk Johnson's death. Don was hit hard by it, hard enough to quit drinking. Clearly he had loved the man, and just as clearly he mourned the passing of the authentic black folk roots of jazz and the blues.

Johnson was another, incidentally, who never did his best, or anywhere near it, in front of a mike. Those who know him today only on the recordings made after World War II, during the New Orleans revival, will wonder why such a to-do was made over so tentative and awkward a musician. The few of us left who heard him in person know he was a first-rate trumpet-player. So was Mutt Carey, another old trumpet-player from Louisiana who was brought to the north during that period by white entrepreneurs and who never performed at his best in the studio.

In about 1948 Don and his wife moved into a flat not far from where I lived. He had a tiny spinet that played with a tinkly sound. Sometimes when I was there I'd unsling my clarinet and we'd play together; that is, we'd try to. Almost always after about eight bars the guy downstairs would start hammering on his ceiling with a broom handle. Sometimes he did it so quickly it seemed as if he must have been waiting there for us to begin. We called him every kind of squarehead and Philistine we could think of. Mostly we called him an asshole.

Once in a while, if we were lucky, the guy downstairs would be out. But it didn't happen often.

Don also had a new record player, a good one for those days, i.e., before hi-fi, and a fair collection of records, including some of the new vinyl discs that sounded so much better than the older ones made from shellac. He had reissues of many important records from the 1920s and 1930s. If we kept the volume low, we could get away with playing them, and since we were young then and had good hearing, this was no hardship. We had a running discussion, in fact more than one, which really had the nature of games, as we knew well enough, because the issues in question could never be resolved. For instance, who was the better clarinetist, Johnny Dodds or Omer Simeon? We played the records over and over again. But although the discussions could rarely settle anything, I emphasize that they were serious, more serious than any literary discussions I've ever heard anywhere. Why? Because underlying them was a deep mutual instinctive response to the music itself, the sounds, the sensory stimuli, such as I think does not exist for partakers in any other art. It was true selfless understanding in the sense given to that term by Schopenhauer, i.e., as opposed to cognition, which is an ego-function. Schopenhauer, the man who first said that all art aspires to the condition of music and that "music is an unconscious exercise in metaphysics in which the mind does not know it is philosophizing"; Don's mind, now that I think of it, was Schopenhauerian. And he was the most intelligent and literate musician I have known.

We played the old records. We listened. We heard. True, they were ten years out of date, some of them more than that, and in jazz a decade is a very long time. We played new records too, of course, but our taste at that time was chiefly for the music of black musicians from Louisiana and the river towns. Don knew many of them, and I knew a few, men like Darnell Howard, Jimmy Yancey, Baby Dodds. The reason we listened so often to the essentially instrumental music of New Orleans was only partly because we liked it. This was classical jazz. (And jazz, we knew, was the classical music of America.) In short, we listened in order to *learn.* Isn't it true that one always learns most from the classics? I believe so. As a poet, I know I can learn something every time I read John Donne's "Canonization," for example, even if it is only the slightest balancing of unaccented syllables in a single line. Just today, as I was driving to the supermarket and playing a tape on my car stereo, I learned something from listening to Zutty Singleton. Granted, he is "old-fashioned" in comparison with the drummers of today; his technique is limited, his style is of his time. But beneath technique and style lies music, the solid foundation. A great rhythmic instinct remains great, no matter when or in whom it appears, and Singleton is great. His work is classic.

Just as I distrust anyone who doesn't love to eat, so I distrust any musician who doesn't love Bach. I've met quite a few who don't, as a matter of fact, though they may protest otherwise. The ones I respect are the others, of whatever sort they may be, jazz musicians, symphonic musicians, even country fiddlers (like Jean Carrignon): when Bach comes on, they shut up and listen.

Often I wonder about the effect of recordings on jazz. Without doubt the evolution of jazz from primitive to extremely sophisticated in less than eighty years has occurred so rapidly because records have distributed the work of important musicians very quickly to everyone, a headlong torrent of invention. When I reflect that only eight years separated the best work of Louis Armstrong (1928) and the recording of "Lady Be Good" by Count Basie, Lester Young, and Buck Clayton, which appeared in 1936 when I was in high school and became virtually the anthem of my generation, I am always—I mean it literally—astonished, the change was so great but the time so brief. And then the first recordings of Charlie Parker in 1942: again the change is almost unbelievable but the time was only eight years. It is as if Aeschylus had come eight years after Homer, instead of five hundred years. Something like that anyway. And of course it has meant a loss. It seems to me that often jazz musicians have been superseded before, even long before, they have explored the resources of their own genius. Many have been pushed into oblivion; others have maintained their reputations and livelihoods by forcibly adapting themselves to new conceptions not accordant with their own understandings. The same thing has happened in literature, of course, and we don't need to use examples from recent times either. Were the esthetic insights that could have been gained from Shakespeare ignored by his successors because his works were printed? They took what they could easily use and stowed the quartos and folios on their shelves. The rapidity of development in English literature from the middle of the sixteenth to the end of the seventeenth century was excessive, and the loss, at least *in potentia,* is evident.

Well, John Keats rediscovered Shakespeare, just as today people are rediscovering, for example, Teddy Wilson, and I am not as disturbed by the acceleration of cultural change as I once was. What would be the point? No one can do anything about it. Besides, we have reasonably accurate editions of Shakespeare precisely because the technology of printing developed coincidentally with the English Renaissance, just as we have actual performances by classical jazz master-artists because the technology of recording coincided with the emergence of jazz. Our gains more than make up for our losses. And there is a further consideration: the real stalwarts of jazz, by which I mean musicians like Coleman Hawkins, Ben Webster, Earl Hines, Vic Dickenson, Red Allen, Pee Wee Russell, Oscar Peterson, Gerry Mulligan, Stan Getz, and a good many others, can keep going for their whole lives in spite of faddistic change, partly by learning from younger musicians (but in sensitively selective ways), and partly from the dynamic propulsion of their own genius. Perhaps the chief characteristic of real genius in the arts is its relentlessness. Those who burn out young, for whatever reason, like John Keats and Charlie Parker, do not give us the solidity of achievement that we have from those who stay the course, like William Shakespeare and Coleman Hawkins.

Beyond this, human sensibility in the larger sense can evolve only so fast, and technology cannot speed it. If, as I believe, the change in human consciousness that characterizes our time in history is as profound as the Renaissance was in Europe, or the apotheosis of love in the ancient world (Plato, the Buddha, Jesus Christ), then apparently such fundamental rearrangements of awareness require about the same length of time no matter when they occur. This is a risky thing to say, I know. The historians may object and ask: "Precisely how long?" Well, several centuries. "Then how do you know that present change, which is certainly not that long, is analogous to others?" Nobody can be sure, of course, but I feel we are only 100-odd years into it, and if the species endures, the change will continue for a long time and in somewhat unpredictable ways. "When did it begin?"

It was customary to say, twenty or thirty years ago when manuals on "existentialism" were being produced for popular consumption, that the change began with Søren Kierkegaard. I would prefer to say with Arthur Schopenhauer. But the difference is unimportant. The change began at about the middle of the nineteenth century, or a little earlier. In any event the recorded beginnings were those worked out by intellectuals in systems of thought based, however obscurely, on prior shifts of social and cultural attitudes that cannot be measured. But let's say the change has been happening for 133 years. Perhaps that means we are halfway through it, or perhaps only a third. How long did the Renaissance last? From Dante to Shakespeare? Only from Petrarch to Ronsard? Copernicus to Bacon? It doesn't matter; you can take whatever chronometry you choose. What matters is the change itself.

If the change in the ancient world was theo-centric, and if that of the Renaissance was anthropo-centric, then the change in our own consciousness is anthropo-eccentric. We are discovering the unimportance and adventitiousness of human existence. Obviously the change does not occur at a uniform rate, and obviously it is still far from "completion." In recent years there has been a distinct counter-change, backward toward some kind of generalized mysticosophy, if I may invent a term; or perhaps this is not backward; but a change is undeniable, its profundity in human consciousness is demonstrable, and its continuance is foreseeable even if not definable.

It used to be called existentialism. Plenty of people today will say that it isn't a real change, that in any case it is over and done with, that the philosophy of *Existenz* is obsolete. In part this is the fault of pseudophilosophers and popularizers, who wrote twenty years ago as if the generation of Sartre, Heidegger, Tillich, Buber, Berdyaev, etc., were a culmination, not a stage in a larger process. I myself felt dismayed ten years ago to see the way young people dismissed the writers and thinkers who had been crucial to my own youthful sense of the world. But I am no longer dismayed, for several reasons:

1. Last year (1982) I offered a graduate course in the works of Albert Camus at Syracuse University. The allotted enrollment was oversubscribed. Only a couple of students had any prior acquaintance with Camus at all, and none had more than the vaguest (usually wrong) ideas about systematic existentialist thought. But in one semester they came not only to understanding and appreciation, but in most cases to eager acceptance of concepts helpful to them in the predicament of their own lives.

2. The popularizers did their work well, and of course were abetted by the course of human affairs in recent years. Today we see the existentialist attitude as a ground for feeling almost

everywhere: in pop music, in such good films as those of Ingmar
Bergman and in thousands of bad ones, in entertainments like
E.L. Doctorow's *Ragtime,* in trashy novels like John Irving's *The
World According To Garp,* and even in the reactive (or anthropo-
dispersive) fantasies of science fiction and *Star Wars.* Millions of
people are living their lives in awareness of the displacement
of human spirit and intelligence, even though they have never
read a philosophical text or experienced a personal confrontation
with the enigma of being and the unimaginableness of nonbeing.
(Hello, Parmenides!) This filtering-down is a necessary part of
change, and when it has received a certain degree of low-level sat-
uration, a new conceptual outgrowth, so to speak, will occur
"at the top" (which I say, I hope, without connotations of élitism).
For the time being, it's true, thoughtful people do wonder if the
concepts of existential "authenticity," "lucidity," "rebellion," etc.,
which were so trenchant thirty years ago, have not been debased
into a kind of pop macho survivalism that is very pervasive and
very depressing. But the tide will turn.

3. Anthropo-eccentric awareness in the past thirty years has
been impacted by the enormous technological disasters of our
time, nuclear physics, devastating environmental pollution, and
all the rest. These are without any doubt powerful reinforcements.
The feeling of apocalypse affects us all. Whether or not this is truly
analogous to the impingement of Copernican astronomy and the
general awakening to the implications of planetary order upon
evolving humanism is something I cannot say with any assurance.
I don't think anyone else can either. But some similarity exists,
and it is interesting, possibly illuminating. Was there acceptance
of knowledge, however painful, followed by control of it? Or was
the new astronomy of the Renaissance merely the beginning of a
cognitive avalanche that has continued ever since and has even-
tuated in our own nuclear jeopardy? I believe some degree of acceptance and control did occur in the Renaissance, and I believe it
was made possible by the underlying change, both intellectual
and popular, in human consciousness that preceded and supported it. Humanism (anthropo-centrism) made the solar system
bearable. And perhaps—just possibly—the existentialist awareness of our time, as it emerges in ever fiercer resistance to massive depersonalization in every sphere, may bring about acceptance and control of knowledge again.

At any rate, if we suppose that the part of reasonableness in our
society is represented in an appreciable degree by the corps of art-

ists, as opposed to the technologists, including especially the technologists of politico-military statism—and I think few people who
are likely to be reading this will deny it—then I see the awareness
of existential attitudes in all our art. I am not referring to self-
conscious exercises in explicit Absurdism, such as Ted Hughes'
Crow, which to my mind are reductive and shallow. I am referring
to the broadest underlying *gestalt* or mind-set that I discern at the
basis of all our poetry, for instance, no matter what the individual
poets profess at a more argumentative level. I see it equally in the
works of Denise Levertov, David Ray, Audre Lord, Ted Berrigan,
Cid Corman, Robert Lowell, Robert Duncan, Allen Ginsberg, Galway Kinnell, Richard Shelton, Etheridge Knight, Adrienne Rich,
Gary Snyder, Diane Wakoski, and James Wright. The list is intentionally miscellaneous, but includes only poets whose work I admire, though in varying degrees. Each poet is representative, I
think, of a different strand in our present literary conspectus,
and we should be grateful for such diversity. (It's worth noting, as
well, that the poetry I definitely do not admire is largely watered
down imitations of one or another of these poets.) All of them are
poets of anthropo-eccentricity; they are poets writing in a condition of existential threat; their work occurs in this context. If the
underlying awareness of what it means to live in a period of en-
larging recognition of human (meaning mental) supervenience
were removed, the work of these poets would become instantly
less meaningful.

Mind, I am speaking of an epoch in the historical sense, almost
in the geological sense: a very large division of human time. I am
not speaking of a style, generation, era; such terms as "classical,"
"romantic," "expressionist," etc., do not apply. And "epoch" brings
to mind "epos," meaning material suitable for treatment in an
epic. We have yet to produce either an American or an existentialist epic, though we have had a few near misses. (I am uncertain what to say of *À la recherche du temps perdu*. It might
qualify. In that case, we need a second, and we need especially an
epic that deals with America and American violence.) In one way
or another the *Cantos, Paterson, Conquistador,* and the works of
American novelists (including Faulkner) all fall short; and so do
the collected films of Charlie Chaplin, although I think they come
closer than anything else. This is the problem of poetry in the
twenty-first century, and it is what our young poets ought to be
thinking about. But I see very little evidence that they are.

Years after Don Ewell and I both left Chicago, we came into touch with each other again, I don't remember quite how. This was in the 1970s. Don was based in Florida, but was working all over the world. We corresponded regularly, and on one of his tours Don came to visit me at my home in rural Vermont. He had had a stroke, and his left arm was partly paralyzed, which meant, for a stride pianist, a real hardship: he had to swing his whole body back and forth in order to play the two-beat bass, and a night of that is truly exhausting. Nevertheless he was playing well, and still with the same devotion of earlier years. He looked awful, much worse than I did, although we were about the same age. A life of hotel rooms, tonks, and planes had taken a heavy toll, whereas my own health, after years of working in the fields and woods, was never better. He slept on the sofa in my living room with the record player turned low and loaded with a stack of Mozart's symphonies. I don't think he slept well. I don't think he ever slept well. To me he seemed the existential man *par excellence.* What better could symbolize the human condition today than the life of an itinerant jazz musician, playing the blues all over the world? The endless sorrow of the music that can never resolve itself. Displacement, traveling, loneliness in the midst of the unrelenting crowd, moments of ecstatic freedom when the imagination soars beyond objectivity and determinism and the perpetual crisis of time. I don't know where Don is now, or if he is still alive. We have fallen out of touch again. But I think of him often, and I play his records often. The truth is, I don't want to know what has become of him. I need him to be, not my alter-ego—horrid technological thought!—but my beckoner to the transcendent reality of the blues, as long as I myself shall last. Because the guy downstairs has taken over the world.

A CHACONNADE
FOR EVERYONE
NAMED REBECCA

For all Rebeccas, yes, but I do have a particular Rebecca in mind, and she is Rebecca Thompson, born two months ago. The reason I have her in mind is this. I have been asked to write about poetry and politics, a topic upon which I have held forth so many times in the past thirty years that now I am discomfited by lack of anything new to say. I am neither a journalist nor a philosopher; I have not the stamina that permits them to go on repeating the same few ideas for a lifetime. Yet the topic is important, it is crucial, and I do not wish to shirk it. Consequently, since my own mind is empty, I choose my point of departure in Rebecca's mind and in the dance of love I find there. Where else is perfect newness, humanly speaking, combined perfectly with the perfect tradition? Rebecca is a fine old name, and I am glad to see it revived.

1. "We live in an age in which the collapse of all previous standards coincides with the perfection in technique for the centralized distribution of ideas; some kind of revolution is inevitable, and will as inevitably be imposed from above by a minority." These words were written in 1933, no matter by whom—he was not the most astute of observers. Anyway the notion was common property among the intelligentsia of the time. In the half-century since then, we have experienced its truth; the revolution has occurred. The minority from above is clearly the corporate will of our commercial megalosaurians; the technique for centralized distribution is clearly electronics; and the "ideas" are clearly our own conditioned responses. The result, as in all revolutions from the right, is massive enslavement. We are a society of weakened mentalities, frightened of true ideas and distrustful of language. A few of us are gripped by a crippling nostalgia for the age of enlighten-

ment, made all the more crippling by our knowledge of the horrendous defects of that age. (Who does not love and hate Mme. Defarge?) A very few of us have such a vision of our present souls as might issue in a program of salvation, which is more than crippling, a paralysis near to death, the evident chance for such salvation being like the eye of the needle. Who is to say whether we should cast our lot with the very few, the few, or the many?

2. At least we have passed beyond the two great questions that agitated poets of the time when the words I have quoted were written, and for some years afterward too. Should poetry stay clear of politics, for fear of pollution? Is politics even a possible topic in the lyric convention, which is all that is left of poetry in the twentieth century? We understand now that the "purity" of poetry is a delusion, and like all delusions is both distractive and debilitating, and we understand also that political poetry is not only feasible in our time but has been splendidly written already by poets whose examples obviate any questions of technique. In short, we have today a broader vision of poetry than was common among poets of the middle part of our century, and we see that the "lyric convention" (though we seldom use that term now) is a freedom, not a restraint.

3. At the same time, unhappily, we see the vision failing. Young poets are aware of it but unable to pursue it. Their poetic sensibilities have been formed from a misappreciation of the autobiographical fashion of recent writing in America, and their poems are formed in the habit of egotism. It is painful to see. In somewhat the same way jazz has devolved from a spontaneous music of coalescing sensibilities into a panorama of linked but separate romantic privileges, though the overriding devotion of even such self-indulgent musicians as Coleman Hawkins and Miles Davis lessens the damage. But in both cases—in *all* cases—the impasse of objective egotism, as distinct from transcendent subjectivity, must be eluded if we are to go forward without disaster in a condition of reality.

4. Yet the habit of egotism has arisen from causes outside art. So I believe, at any rate, and the belief constitutes a grain—not of hope, which I some time ago abjured—but of optimism, a glint of light in the immense darkness of futurity. The failure of young poets comes from their maleducation, a huge cultural dysfunction that certainly is not limited to the schools—if it were, we should have a good chance of reform—but is pervasive and is found perhaps under its most excruciating aspect in the very cen-

ter of the American myth, by which I mean "the home." Poems are written for love. Poems have always been written for love. Young poets who are unable to scan Shakespeare, who are unable to re-act to any language more expressive than journalese, can hardly be expected to *hear* the concerned intention of great poetry; but even if these interpretive skills were somehow, miraculously, in-jected into them, young poets would still be young Americans, which is to say, sensibilities deformed by the whole range of social environment that offers nothing but images of fraud, fear, sen-sory mollification, meaningless words, and rewarded infamy. No wonder the young poet does not know what to do with his ves-tigial esthetic impulse and superincumbent political fear. "What's more, as a failure, a superfluous man, a neurasthenic, and victim of the times, anything is permitted him." So wrote Chekhov. His-tory as usual proffers us confirmations of our tabescence. And what is permitted the young poet today is to go to university, the seat of intellectual desuetude, and there to join fellow poets in the pretense that unusual line-endings and ingenious metaphors make good poems.

5. A decade ago people often asserted that all human acts are political. It is true. It is, in fact, a truism, in spite of the desire of the modernist poets, notably T.S. Eliot, to emphasize the im-prisonment of the individual soul: no hermitage can be so private that it severs the connectedness of humanity. But ten years ago the truism, extended from Aristotle's definition of man as the po-litical animal, was usually uttered in anger, since that was a pe-riod of social vitality and social vitality is always a manifestation of anger. Moreover anger is useful, it is probably essential. (I am writing in anger at this moment, if anyone didn't know.) But an-ger has its risks, chief of which is its impediment to clear seeing. I think the political poets of the period of social vitality did not suf-ficiently understand that politics is love, anger is love, and poetry is love. *All human acts are loving, one way or another.* The defi-cient awareness of love among most, though by no means all, an-gry poets of ten or fifteen years ago is one reason why their poems fail to hold the imaginations of young poets today.

6. Think of the state of mind of Rebecca, who has so recently come forth in the world, bringing with her our old and only specifi-cally human capacity, which is to love. This is not Wordsworthian mystical obscurantism. On the contrary, it is all that I can prag-matically conceive: the psychological development of the human foetus can be nothing, in that marvelous environment, but a

growth of love. Granted, a shattering begins at the moment of birth, and love thereafter gradually disperses into its numerous constituent elements, including anger. (This, I take it, is the meaning of the story of Pandora's box, the pun being fundamental.) But at two months, as all heeding parents know, the infant's emotive capacities are still pretty well integrated, still almost totally loving. Because of this she is beautiful.

7. What an act of daring it is to project oneself into Rebecca's mind, or as some would say, to reduce oneself to her "mental level." Yet daring is not so hard. Really it's quite easy, a psychological trick. I learned it long ago, and I am well aware that nothing in my work or life has made me exceptional in this respect. How else could I be writing this, which is so ridiculous to the world?

8. Another quotation: "Even young children understand and love distinction of soul, because it speaks from mind to mind and gives them confidence in the world." That is by Joyce Cary. (The quote under no. 1 above is from W.H. Auden.)

9. At the beginning I said that Rebecca's mind is a dance of love. Maybe it is a poem. Maybe its mode is not to be differentiated. But one thing is certain: it is an act of the imagination. What else does she possess to go with her five little wits? Another thing is certain too: it is a political act. She has not yet conceived more than the vaguest hint of loneliness. She is steadfastly directed toward the other. If young poets were to ask my advice in these times of weakness and demoralization, which they mostly don't, I would say to them: "Become Rebeccas. Let the fragments of love be reassembled in you. Only then will you have true courage. And after that? Well, you know the techniques, you know the differences between poetry and propaganda—or if you don't, you can easily learn them. And then you will write political poetry in spite of yourselves."

FREEDOM AND DISCIPLINE

Saint Harmony, many
years I have stript

naked in your service
under the lash. Yes,

I believe the first
I heard (living, there

aloud in the hall) was
Sergei Rachmaninoff

set at the keys like a
great dwarf, a barrel

on three spindles,
megalocephalus, hands

with fourteen fingers,
ugly as Merlin, with whom

I was in love, a boy and
an old man; a boy nodding

and an old man sorrowing
under the bushfire of the

people's heart, until he
coolly knocked out the

Prelude in C♯ Minor. Second
was Coleman Hawkins

in about 1933 perhaps.
I, stript and bleeding,

leapt to the new touch,
up and over the diminished

in a full-voiced authority
of blue-gold blues. I

would do nothing, locked
in discipline, sworn to

freedom. The years shrieked
and smothered, like billboards

beside a road at night.
I learnt how Catlett

drove the beat without
harming it, how Young

sped between the notes,
how Monk reconstructed

a broken chord to make
my knuckles rattle, and much

from oblivion: Newton,
Fasola, Berigan, my

inconsolable Papa Yancey.
Why I went to verse-making

is unknowable, this
grubbing art. Trying,

Harmony, to fix your beat
in things that have none

and want none—absurdity!
Let that be the answer

to any hope of statecraft.
As Yeats said, *Fal de rol.*

Freedom and discipline concur
only in ecstasy, all else

is shoveling out the muck.
Give me my old hot horn.

ACADEMICISM

"De la musique avant toute chose. . . ." With these words Paul Verlaine began his *Art poétique,* which he wrote in 1874 and published a decade later. What admirable directness! Verlaine, who in his life must be accounted among the most miserable of men, nevertheless had a steady, forthright mind. In their musicality, which is all some readers can apprehend, his lyric poems were composed with an acuity of conception that eluded Poe or Lanier or Swinburne or anyone else—except Stéphane Mallarmé.

And so in a century we have come half circle. In the tedious *ars poetica* which I see being constructed in our literary reviews today, the music of poetry is the last consideration, if indeed it has not been banished altogether.

Not the least of my existential disaffections is the fact that my life has been lived during a time when all public attitudes were swinging near to the end of the pendulum's arc.

Verbal effect of whatever kind, conventional or original, is distractive: so I have been told hundreds of times. A poem is a structure of images, of metaphors, of cultural conventions, of experiential mediations, of free associations, i.e., of anything but language. Language is a bugaboo; get rid of it. If the poet is stuck with language anyway, as is obviously the case, then let it be merely notative or, better, transparent; that is, a sign pointing toward the real, inexpressible inner poem, or a lens revealing it. Indicator or opener, never the thing itself. The poem is a synapse, and poetry is a mystique.

A mundane mystique, however. To be fair to my friends who tell me my songs are too poetic, they are not believers in Kenneth Rexroth's vaticitude.

Often in the past I have written that good criticism must be subjective. But I did not mean solipsistic. Subjectivity is what transcends objectivity, which is the world of the ego, the mirror.

Before I began teaching, i.e., three years ago, I should have thought that the workshop would engender an attitude of receptiveness. In the workshops that I myself have conducted—or that have conducted me—I have found students of very different temperaments and opinions, and I have learned that my job consists primarily in educing a rapport in which these conflicting temperaments and opinions can act with mutual benefit. But in the larger conspectus I see none of this. I see only poets and critics whose objective egos have become systematized in doctrine. I see only prejudgment and prescription.

Academicism is the specialization of partiality. It is the opposite to seeking the intention that each work of art projects for itself, in order then, and only then, to estimate the degree of fulfillment. And this specialization infects artists quite as much as scholars.

Somewhere the poet James Wright once "translated" the opening line of *Art poétique*, with perfect justice, as: "Solitude before all else." (I quote from memory.) In art the expressive is the sensual. In poetry the sensual is rhyme and meter, using these terms in the broadest sense. If the sensual is removed, only information or "airy nothing" remains, either of which may be conveyed in computer language without a loss. But the sensual may be apprehended only in the body's privacy. "L'art, mes enfants, c'est d'être absolument soi-même," wrote Verlaine elsewhere, and by "absolument soi-même" he meant the transcendent subjectivity, not the ego. The absolute self in poetry is what creates and responds to rhyme and meter, the sensual, the expressive. I would almost propose that the amount of inexpressive poetry is always in precise inverse ratio to the lack of absolute selfhood.

Absolute selfhood is neither vain nor humble, for these are qualities solely of the reactive ego in the objective world.[1]

Since we have no shortage of talent, the academy without academicism would be wonderful, perhaps what Yvor Winters had in mind years ago when he recommended the life of the university as a good one for poets. Yet Winters, as true a man and poet as you can expect to find, himself fell prey to the specialization of partiality. His criticism is full of it. I wonder if the academy without academicism is possible. Perhaps the specialization of partiality is a necessary component of any corporatism or collectivism, especially in our historical era. More broadly, can a church endure without churchliness? Not, at any rate, as long as competition, the rivalry of egos, in all its ugliness and inexpressiveness prevails.

NOTE

1. These remarks are extended from the idea offered in my essay called "The Act of Love" (*Working Papers,* Athens, Ga., 1982, pp. 219–29).

WHO CARES,
LONG AS IT'S B-FLAT

Floyd O'Brien, Teagardens Charlie & Jack
    where are the snowbirds of yesteryear?

Boyce Brown, Rod Cless, Floyd Bean
    Jimmy McPartland, Danny Polo
Hank Isaacs, Davy Tough, Jim Lannigan

    where are you, Jim Lannigan?

Jesus but you were awful musicians
    Pee Wee, Abby, and you Faz
awful awful. Can you please
    tell me the way to Friar's Point?

"Aw, Jess." "Shake it, Miss Chippie, but don't
    break it."
"Listen at that dirty Mezz!" Can you
    tell me please
the way to White City? Where
    can I find
the Wolverines, Teschemacher?

    Leon Rappolo?

Eubie, Punch, Darnell? "Cut him
    Mister Reefer Man." "I wisht
    I had a barrel of it."

Muggsy, Muggsy where art thou
   where is Pinetop
where are the Yanceys now?

35 years
   swish-swish of a velvet cymbal
   twinkling leaves
in the lilac tree

"When I die
       when I die
              please bury me

sweet mamo
        in a sardine can . . ."

Coda
  And these little cats think
    they discovered something

              (*gawd*

damm)

INFLUENCES:
THE FORMAL IDEA
OF JAZZ

Tracking influences has become an old game by now. We have had plenty of time to see its limitations and absurdities. If I say, for instance, that during the period when I first devoted myself seriously and searchingly to metrical composition, the poets whose works I read the most were Ben Jonson, William Yeats, and Ezra Pound, the statement is true but meaningless. The real question is not by whom I was influenced, but how. The crudest distinction would be between reactive and imitative, I suppose. Did I steal from the masters or reject them? The answer is undiscoverable, for which I am thankful. And even if one could find it, it would still need to be compounded incalculably with dozens of lesser influences, including those exerted on me by my own friends and contemporaries.

Then the further likelihood that the most important influences were not those impinging directly on my poems but those that came much earlier. Mother Goose, the songs of Shakespeare, *The Ingoldsby Legends,* Byron, Stephen Foster, the poets I read in school, Longfellow, Whittier, Tennyson, and scores of others, perhaps hundreds of others. They came to me at the time when I wrote poems only as a kind of children's game. They entered the inchoate sensibility of a struggling child in twisted ways that can never be unraveled. And again I am thankful.

A poem my father wrote for me when I was two years old was such a favorite of mine that he copied it out in a fair hand and framed it and hung it on the wall. The first line ran, "There was a little duck and he went quack, quack." I can say now, nearly a lifetime later, that I am ashamed to have forgotten the rest of it, ashamed that I do not know what happened to the framed manuscript.

A couple of years ago I read an article by a scholar who had found about a dozen "reduplicated" phrasings in *The Faerie Queene* and the works of Alexander Pope. The article was interesting and even slightly shocking; we think of Pope as being remote from Spenser in every way, so that the two must fall into separate categories. Yet we know that Pope was a precocious child, that he read widely, that indeed by the time he was twelve years old he probably had read every poem accessible to him in English, to say nothing of French, Latin, Greek, etc. It would be folly to think that such a person, living in that time, could have avoided the Spenserian epic, or that the poem would not have left a deep impression, though who knows in what complex, conflicting, and hidden ways?

Complex and conflicting. That is almost as much as I can say about the literary influences on my own writing. What remains is that I was, during much of my life, pathologically uncentered in both style and personality, and that I freely took on the styles and personalities of others. Even at my present age, nearly sixty, I see no clearly identifiable center in the existence, poetic or other, of Hayden Carruth, that stranger. Not long ago I had occasion to study the works of Paul Goodman with care, and immediately I began to write poems in his peculiar and lovely syntax. Thirty years ago I might have been embarrassed by such anxious mimicry. Now I simply say that I am grateful to Paul for showing me a new means by which to express some of the troubles that have recently been on my mind.

And that is the end of it, provided we restrict ourselves to "literary" influences. What is more important, however, yet at the same time more difficult to discuss, is the influence on writing of the other arts; in my case particularly the influence of jazz. I have always insisted that the connections among the arts are nonformal, at best tenuous; and many people have complained about my editorial prejudice against mixed *genres*. The "art" of collage seems to me intrinsically self-contradictory. I dislike poems about paintings or pieces of music. Then what can I say about the influence of jazz on poetry? In fact there *is*, as we all empirically know, some functional analogy among the arts, and the problem is to define it, to discriminate precisely what can be transmitted from one artistic medium to another. I scarcely know how to attempt it.

An immediate difficulty arises from the fact that human beings are divided into two parts: a great majority that cannot experience jazz as music; a minority that can and does. Every member of the minority will know what I'm talking about. I don't know how many times—but over the years a great many—someone has come into my home, proclaimed his or her devoted enthusiasm for jazz—"Oh, I just *love* Billie Holiday," etc.—and has asked me to put a record on the phonograph, only to begin, after the first eight bars, talking a blue streak that lasts till the record ends, by which time the topic of music has been long forgotten. It is infuriating. I am one who must have complete silence when music is playing; a small clash of cutlery from the next room, a dog barking somewhere down the road, can wipe out a vertical moment of sound (be it a solo piano or a full orchestra and chorus) and utterly destroy the passage in question. It was bad enough in the remote hills where I used to live. In the crude and graceless city where I live now, sirens never cease to wail, trucks to roar, plumbing to flush. But of all the sounds that destroy music, the human speaking voice is worst.

Some people can hear jazz, and others, by far the greater number, cannot. The worst poem Dr. Williams ever wrote was "Ole Bunk's Band" (I give the title from memory), in which he treats Bunk Johnson and the other old-time musicians playing with him as if they were some unintelligible anthropological specimens, people from another and distant culture making noises for the mere hell of it or out of animal exuberance. That they were artists like him never crossed his mind. Delmore Schwartz, thirty years ago when he and I used to drink on Tuesday afternoons at a bar on Madison Avenue, could talk rings around me about baseball, although I was not unknowledgeable; but when it came to jazz, which he professed to love, he could not speak except in sociological terms: "this outpouring of racial misery," "phenomenon of human expression in industrial society," etc. I sighed (but only to myself).

This has nothing, incidentally, to do with being tone deaf. I know musicians trained in the European tradition who perform flawlessly and even imaginatively when they are reading a score by Mozart or Ravel but who cannot hear the musical qualities of jazz.

I do not say—and please note this well—that incalculably many social, historical, cultural, and other external values do not adhere to jazz. On the contrary, no art exists in a vacuum. But I do say that this is definably a question of adherence and not of intermixture. The music itself, the continuum of textured sounds and rhythms, is "pure." It cannot in itself contain or express any ideational substance, and even emotional substance—leaving aside titles, lyrics, and all other cultural adherents—can only be suggested through psychic analogy, a term I have just invented and do not care to try to amplify. Hence I conclude, equally unscientifically, that some people innately possess a sensory apparatus somehow capable of apprehending jazz as music, and that other people do not. Those in the former group will perfectly understand what I am writing here; they already know it in their own experience. To the rest, who may or may not be musically inclined but who lack the capacity to respond to the distinctive sensual qualities of jazz, what I have written so far will seem arbitrary and perhaps élitist, though that is not my intention at all, and what I shall attempt to write now will seem puzzling and inconsequential.

Nevertheless and in spite of the philosophical and verbal difficulties implicit in any attempt to discuss crossovers among the arts—difficulties so great that some estheticians deny the possibility—I want to write something, if I can, about the influence of jazz as jazz upon my poetry as poetry, hoping thereby to illuminate the vexing enigma of influences in general.

I shan't attempt what so many who are more competent than I have tried and failed to do, namely, to define jazz at the same time completely and distinctly. Our vocabularies, even our technical ones and even for that matter our nonverbal systems of notation, are inadequate. Every characteristic of jazz to which the critics point can be found in other musics. The business about coming in ahead of or behind the beat, for instance, often only a hairsbreadth away from it: doubtless this accounts in part for the swinging quality of jazz. But the same manner of performance can be found in gypsy music, flamenco, African and Oriental music, and others; while some jazz musicians have attained the same propulsive force by playing almost nothing but eighth notes, each one squarely on the beat—Boyce Brown, the mad monk of Chicago in the late twenties and early thirties, being an extreme example, though in the early period of bop, Parker, Gillespie, Peterson, and many others were doing essentially the same thing. Moreover it is undeniable that a swinging, propulsive quality is just as prominent in Bach, Scott Joplin, and the Rolling Stones as it is in jazz, although the former all composed and performed in standard, predictable, easily measurable and notatable rhythmic patterns.

It is the same with texture. Many inexperienced listeners used to think that raucous instrumental tone was the main ingredient of jazz, a belief upon which the entrepreneurs of pop culture—

Clyde McCoy, the owners of the Cotton Club, Sophie Tucker, thousands of others—capitalized mightily. This belief has somewhat diminished, I think. But it is true without question that jazz instrumentalists have enlarged the textural capacities of their instruments beyond anything conceivable a century ago. What Coleman Hawkins, Lester Young, Ben Webster, Buddy Tate, Sonny Rollins, John Coltrane, and scores of others have done with the tenor saxophone could not have occurred in the wildest, most delightful fantasies of Antoine Sax, who invented the instrument (i.e., the "family" of instruments) less than a century before many of these musicians had become masterful stylists. But the real point is that textural expressiveness is part of *all* music; we cannot think of any music, or play it to ourselves inside our heads, without awareness of texture. Often people say that the themes of J.S. Bach are so pure that they can be played on any instrument without loss. But this is true only so long as one considers the music solely as a structure of tones; substitute a vibraphone for the harpsichord in the fifth Brandenburg concerto and see if the effect, the expressiveness, is not much altered. When it comes to Purcell, Boccherini, Berlioz, or Debussy, and when it comes to traditional Japanese or Arabic music, the case is plain. Instrumental textures, and for that matter vocal textures, are as various as can be, and throughout the world are regarded not as adjuncts to the particular music in question but as inseparable and integral parts of it.

Finally, the slur. Everyone knows that jazz performers commonly do not hit a note with true pitch but slide into it from below or above; the same when the note tails off. Slurs, glides, intentional muffs and clinkers are conspicuous. Some musicians—Rex Stewart, Pee Wee Russell—have made false notes a deliberate part of their work. Granted, most musicians in the European tradition of the conservatories have regarded untrue pitch as anathema; yet a few knew the value of slurs—Paganini, Mahler, Ravel. And if we turn to other musics—the regional folk musics of Europe, the Chinese opera, and doubtless the shepherd's airs of Pan (for I believe the shawm, easy to slur, was likelier his instrument than the syrinx)—the point needs no further arguing.

I have dwelt on these qualities of jazz for one reason: to isolate them categorically and exclude them from further consideration. These along with other such properties are the essences of jazz, the musical values, without which there could be no jazz. They have deeply affected my writing, and I could search through my books to find examples that would illustrate such substantial analogies, passages of rhythmic, textural, and tonally modulative verbalisms—the extrinsic embodiments. But then so could someone else find these same things in his or her poetry, someone who knows nothing about jazz. How can I prove that my composition comes from jazz? I can't. I can only assert, as I do, that the verbal qualities of my poetry bear a close resemblance to the musical qualities of jazz, which have been powerful influences on me since the age of ten or eleven, and that I believe the best reader of my poetry will probably be a person who knows and loves jazz as I do. But maybe not. And in any event the question is indemonstrable.

What is more important to me than the essence of jazz is its formal idea. I must be careful here; the definition is difficult but necessary. But I believe the idea, in the Platonic sense, of jazz is spontaneous improvisation within a fixed and simple form, usually improvisation by more than one musician at a time, even if the ensemble comprises no more than a solo instrument and a rhythm section. (Though in fact good jazz of the kind that consists of successive solo improvisations, i.e., the mode that has been dominant for some decades, will be a linear evolution of themes and ideas involving all musicians of the ensemble, each in turn. It is as if the true ensemble improvisation of earlier jazz had been separated into its parts and performed consecutively. Thus the soloist improvises for and with fellow musicians and selected other auditors, just as the poet writes for and with fellow poets and selected other readers.) I do not mean to say that elements of convention and artifice are not operative in jazz; they obviously are; but the idea of spontaneous improvisation within a fixed, simple form has been present from the start (say, circa 1910) and has become only more and more dominant since then. This is common knowledge.

What happens, subjectively and spiritually, when a musician improvises freely? He transcends the objective world, including the objectively conditioned ego, and becomes a free, undetermined sensibility in communion with others equally free and undetermined. Long ago I wrote, in a poem about jazz, the following couplet:

> Freedom and discipline concur
> only in ecstasy.

Taken from its context in the poem, this may seem an extravagant statement; yet it is my belief, it is my lifelong conviction. Freedom and discipline are both required, but they cannot be had separately, nor can they be had in the objective world that not only separates them but puts them into conflict. Hence my best poems have all been written in states of transcendent concentration and with great speed. Even my long poems break down into parts composed in this way. And all have been composed within the limits of a fixed and simple form, as fixed and simple as the chord changes of the traditional twelve-bar blues. Sometimes I have used the standard conventions of English prosody, at others I have (more musically) run my phrasing ad lib over a predetermined number of beats to the line, and occasionally I have used alliterative or syllabic meters. But always in my good writing, as I judge it, I have interfused thematic improvisation and metrical regularity or, as I prefer to say, metrical predictability. My less than good writing contains many attempts in which this interfusion failed for any of almost countless untraceable reasons, and also many so-called free form poems. Not one of the latter has ever satisfied me.

It goes without saying that style is another question. A percussionist may play like either Jo Jones or Max Roach. In general I prefer jazz that is stylistically reticent, probably because I am a man of my own generation and can't change that. The steady unostentatious beat of Jo Jones or Sid Catlett, with only an occasional rimshot or acciaccatura to accent or counteraccent the improvised melody, is my model, and I usually hope—but not always, because sometimes one wants technique to be the substance of one's poem—my use of regular measure and rhyme will be unnoticed by the reader. I suppose what I really hope is that these elements *will* be noticed, but then forgotten quickly in the onrush of other components, i.e., the overriding improvisation. In my best poems I think—though how can one know?—this is what happens.

And now I hear someone protesting: "But jazz is an urban phenomenon, or at least has been for the past forty years, and you are a poet of the rural scene." Yes. But the contradiction is apparent, not real. In fact I have heard as much jazz, one way or another, during my years in the hills of Vermont as I did thirty years ago when I lived in New York City. And if I haven't been able to perform with others, I have spent as much time as ever woodshedding (in my case sometimes literally) with my horn. The spontaneous act can occur anywhere, and discipline once learned does not depart.

The textural, rhythmic, and tonally modulative qualities of jazz can apply as well to my love of natural beauty and my love of women, and to the moral, psychological, and metaphysical agonies arising from these loves, as they can apply to another poet's more urban and artificial experience.

(Further, for the past year and a half I have been living in an urban environment myself, and if I can write any more at all I expect my poems will begin to reflect the change before long.)

Then, of course, a more fundamental reason for the pervasive influence of jazz in my writing, whatever my themes or feelings, comes to the surface. Freedom and discipline are the perennial and universal conditions for artistic creation; they are the two pillars on which all esthetics stand. What I have written here is less a statement than a restatement, the primary elements of which can be found in critical attempts from all the times and places ever inhabited, so to speak, by human inquiry. But jazz gives us a new angle of vision, a new emphasis, and this is important too. The past sixty years of jazz have produced an eruption of both individual and correlative genius that is truly astounding, and because of the nature of jazz this has placed the emphasis in creative intuition precisely where it should be, on the fusion of "tradition and the individual talent," on the concurrence of discipline and freedom, and on the mutuality of creative transcendence. I say, let us rejoice. We have little enough otherwise to please us.

Some years ago I wrote in a biographical note which was published in an anthology that if I'd had my choice I would have been a musician. Some people have objected: "You are the opposite to that type, you are so quiet," etc. Well, there has been no shortage of reflective minds among jazz performers, nor of any other type either. We should know from the histories of all the arts that genius is where it is, unpredictable. For myself, I know my sensibility was better attuned to jazz than to any other artistic mode; but the rest of my personality was unfit for it. Perhaps that accounts in part for the sorrow that appears to emanate from the center of my poems. The truth is, whether for good or ill and to the extent—is it any at all?—that we enjoy freedom of choice in this world, poetry for me was, and is, second-best to jazz.

JOE TURNER

Called him "Big Joe" yes and Joe Turner it was his name
And he sang yes he sang
                                well them deep down country blues
With a jump-steady and a K.C. beat   that came
From his big old heart and his bouncing shoes
From that big old bouncing voice

Baby, you so beautiful and you gotta die someday

                                 the same
As those Kansas City nights   huge boozy flame
Of the miserloos and the careless joys /   But slow
He could sing it too when it took him   sorrow
In the bone   slow

    Broken the ten commanmint,
    Beat out with the jinx,
    Can't sometimes
    Get water to drink,
    Ain't got a mount to jack in,
    Can't produce a dime,
    I'm jus as raggdy
    As a jay-bird in whistlin ti—
                          ime———

                                 over and over
In the gathering of souls the flickering
Of human destiny that sways to discover

Happiness in fate.   And it was music, music.
"Shouter," they called him. And great is what he was,
Warm and   reckless   and accurate and   big—

Saint Harmonie,
          touch thou these lines with Turner's voice.

SONG ABOUT EARL HINES

"Turn out all the lights
   and call the law
right now." And it's true, it's veridical, he had that raw
   necessary animal spirit and enjoyed a hell of a
good time all those nights

of his life, yet you can't hear and not know
   how he studied to make his left hand do
those rhythmic variations, how he began
   new musics again and again. "Oh Father Hines, you
dirty old man."

WITH RESPECT TO
THE INFURIATING
PERVASIVENESS OF
OPTIMISM

When Ezra Pound was a young man, he assumed his intellectual character in a phase of Anglican culture created by one man, Matthew Arnold. When Pound went to London in 1910, he landed in an Arnoldian *milieu*. These are, I imagine, sufficiently extravagant generalizations, which is what I intend them to be. I am not speaking of Pound the poet, the student of comparative literature, the technical innovator, and so on. I am speaking rather of Pound the exemplary figure, the young intellectual among other intellectuals, who took on unavoidably and unconsciously the optimism of the nineteenth century's greatest English arbiter of cultural understanding.

But Arnold was no feather-brain. He was a poet. He was also a critic, an educator, a public administrator, and a hardheaded practical man. He had functioned imaginatively in precise reaction against the Byronesque romanticism that had lingered in English sensibility beyond the middle of the century. Nor was Arnold a utopian in any sense, being distinct in this from many of his great contemporaries, Ruskin, Morris, Marx, Spencer, Darwin, and others. Arnold was, if you like, the Grand Reformer, the exponent of Liberalism Writ Large; and his attraction for later generations, perhaps especially in the U.S.A. (Eliot included him among the luminaries of Cousin Harriet's parlor library), was his essential pragmatism, even his cultural relativism, and his disdain for ideological thought in general, whether Positivist or Tractarian.

Yet Matthew Arnold was the one who said that art is "a criticism of life," and what could be more optimistic than that? In his work the idea of criticism became almost ideological; it acquired an expansiveness and aggressiveness it had never had before, making it truly functional and directive, not in a Johnsonian or didactic manner, but expressly in and through the imagination. Art became criticism, and criticism became art, in both senses of "becoming." Thus artists were not only recorders of change in human affairs, they were moderators and mediators. They could be and should be assessors, instigators, and moral henchmen.

Arnold was the Aristotle of the modern world, at least in the parts of it that speak English.

When Pound became an old man, he fell into a deep depression. I ignore for the present whatever biographical, read pathological, factors may have induced it. "I can't make it cohere," he said. And since he was decidedly a human being he took his failure personally. Yet what in the *Cantos* themselves requires such a failure? When I think about that huge poem, though I find parts of it odious, I see nothing that could not have been structured systematically by an imagination as inventive as Pound's. No, the incoherence lay not in the elements of the poem but in the world.

Pound was born in 1885, three years before my father. Both men lived from the world of Arnold into the world of the hydrogen bomb. What Pound had begun in cultural optimism could not be sustained beyond Hiroshima. Optimism gave way, the idea of coherence gave way, the poem gave way. My father, though he wrote no big poems, wrote little ones, and he too, like who knows how many others of that generation, ended in the silence of despair, so bitter that his not speaking was a kind of incandescence.

Someone will no doubt suggest that Pound was saturated with the tragic view and that this cannot be equated with optimism. But I believe—I have come to believe, having all my life studied and leaned heavily upon the tragic view—just the contrary. The tragic view of life and art, which pits human intelligence against the incoherence of fate and celebrates, however negatively, the authenticity, solidity, and *value* of human experience, this tragic view, I believe, from Sophocles to Shakespeare to Schopenhauer to Sartre, is at bottom not only a mode of optimism but essentially more optimistic, not less, than the progressivism of Hegel and Whitman and Henry Ford, to say nothing of Plato. Yet a work begun in the optimism of tragedy is self-contradictory. It must admit failure in the face of incoherence in order to make its point. It becomes a comedy, what we call a black comedy. And I am by no means the first to point out that the *Cantos*, like *King Lear*, are comedic.

Is optimism then an inevitable component of any constructive human effort, meaning effort aimed at change? Is it a part of human "nature"? Perhaps it is. (And let's avoid the riddle of what, if anything, human nature means.) My own historical imagination suggests to me, however, that another mode is possible, a mode in which optimism is not present at all, either positively or negatively, a mode in short based upon the antemodern belief that time is linear and eternity is circular. If I look at the mind of Dante and compare it with the mind of Descartes, I see that at some point between them linearity became progress and circularity became utopianism—striking variances. And to my mind it is by no means incidental that the *Divina Commedia* is a good deal more coherent than the *Discours de la méthode*.

As for myself, I have come to the age of sixty-two, and in considering the failure of my own work, I am struck, not for the first time but now very forcibly, by the extent to which my life has been lived in the Poundian mold. I mean unintentionally as well as intentionally. (But I do *not* mean ideologically, in case anyone should think otherwise.) In my writing, but even more in my work as editor, reviewer, and general entrepreneur, I have been imbued, though I am temperamentally, read pathologically, as solemn and forlorn a creature as anyone would care to meet, with Arnoldian optimism. I am my father's son, as well as Pound's. I and my friends believed we were still part of a beleaguered avant-garde, and we had good reason for that belief in 1945. Such poets as Pound, Williams, and Cummings were still unable to find publishers, still utterly unknown to educators. We thought that if we could shift the focus of American culture, especially in the schools, away from the line of taste established in Cambridge, Mass., in 1870, then we could effect a real and significant change in our civilization. Well, we succeeded. We succeeded to such an extent that we are now almost rueful, seeing that children no longer read *Evangeline* or "I Must Go Down to the Sea Again" and that Ph.D. dissertations are now being written on the poetry of Howard Nemerov, for God's sake! And has American civilization changed? Yes, but only in the direction that was evident, all too evident, forty years ago. It has gotten worse.

At any rate this is how the problem presents itself to me now. The efficacy of art, if there is to be any, must depend on some truly fundamental change in consciousness. On this matter it is hard not to think backwards. Gary Snyder would say, I believe, "Let's regress to the purity of the animals." Clayton Eshleman, "Let's get back to the Aurignacians." Wendell Berry, "The essential values and practical techniques are to be found in a peasant culture." And so on. To my mind any such nostalgia is flawed by the historical delusion of Unprogress, which is just as bad as Progress. It is a type of sentimentality; reduced to doctrine, it is the motive of the reactionary State. For what has been done cannot be undone, and we can look only forward, whether we like it or not; that is, to tomorrow or the day after tomorrow, but never beyond our own lives, since that would be the sentimentality of utopian progress and the motive of the progressive State. (Is not our unsentimental tomorrow the basis of the tragic view?) We must enter—soon!—a phase of consciousness beyond—well, I do not know what word to use here, and I must resort to jargony wordmaking in the style of the politicians—hence, beyond implementalism. Writers must be authors, not agents. Authorship, not agency, is our service. Note the difference well.

What are the alternatives? Several, I suppose. Certainly one is the horrid game of literary politics, so empty and fatuous, which we primarily associate with New York City, though it is played everywhere. The game is ruled by greed, of course; but its impetus and energy come from an attempt to escape the failure of optimism, which is to say, an attempt to prolong the Arnoldian tragic view, coherence embattled within incoherence, in spite of the Poundian *débâcle*.

Some of my friends will be snickeringly surprised by what they perceive as a turn toward religion in these remarks. Others will think just the contrary and will say, "Aha! See how he leans toward the Deconstructionists." But myself, I am not surprised. For one thing, both elements have been present in my mind and work for many years, although the tasks I undertook prevented them from being developed or emphasized; for another, I am confident neither will emerge in a doctrinal orientation.

Now another alternative occurs to me, in addition to game-playing. It is the kind of criticism that Arnold would have applauded; I mean criticism that exhibits itself as a system, sometimes even as a program. Critics like Hugh Kenner and Richard Ellmann, who believe they can produce a work that is, however circumscribed, not only coherent but comprehensive, are perhaps the greatest, most deluded optimists of all. Their counterparts among poets are those who, like Francis Ponge, insist that one can achieve an exact, complete description of one's big toe, or

at any rate that it is worth dying in the attempt to do so. As for
me my excuse, if I need one, for packing such huge and crudely
drawn concepts into this brief essay is that I think no other way is
possible. I take my leave of the whole shebang. I decline optimism
in all its forms at last.

But is it optimistic to believe I have the choice?

A POSSIBLY
MOMENTARY DECLARATION
IN FAVOR OF
WILLIAM BUTLER YEATS AND
CHARLES ELLSWORTH RUSSELL

He was called Pee Wee. A silly name, especially since he was taller than average, though it would have been silly in any case, a name I don't care for. But that is how he is known to thousands upon thousands of people ignorant of his real name, yet aware—many of them—of his genius and his importance in the development of jazz. Here at the beginning I must use his nickname once in order to identify him.

The first time I heard Russell was in 1937 or 1938, I can't remember exactly. But it must have been not long after Nick Rongetti opened his club on Sheridan Square in the Village. Nick's, it was called. Like all such dives, it pressured its customers mercilessly to spend as much as possible, the waiters and bartenders pushing drinks without letup and clearly bored by the music. So were many of the customers, who came only for the "atmosphere." I was in high school then, but unfortunately—at any rate for my incipient alcoholism—I could pass for a man of twenty-five, especially when I was with older people. For once, however, I was not much interested in the booze. I drank my weak gin-and-Cokes because they were the price of admission, and I concentrated, to the exclusion of everything else, the bustle, the idiotic conversation, etc., on the music.

Who were the musicians? Russell, of course; I remember him with perfect recall, his extraordinary grimaces when he was playing, his withdrawnness when he was not. Also Brad Gowans on valve trombone. He waved his horn somewhat imperiously in front of him as he strolled back and forth on the edge of the bandstand, playing the fast descending runs that distinguished him from other trombonists. George Wettling was at drums; I recall him clearly too. The rest are hazier; probably Bobby Hackett playing cornet, though it might have been Max Kaminsky; Joe Bushkin or Frank Signorelli, probably the former, at the piano; perhaps Israel Crosby on bass. And of course Eddie Condon, who sat there whanging his guitar, though I always tended, then and later, to discount him on the grounds that he had nothing whatever to do with the happenings on the stand, i.e., what was coming out of the heads of the other musicians.

I had not heard much live jazz at that time, almost none; nor much recorded jazz either, for that matter. I did not have money to buy a record player, though sometimes I bought records anyway and laid them away like treasure for the time when I would be able to play them. I lived in a genteel, lower-middle-class village about thirty miles north of Manhattan, a place I despised and from which my attempts to escape were totally ineffectual. No matter; it was probably no worse than anywhere else. I did have a radio, a stand-up model with splintered veneer and frayed cloth over the speaker that I had salvaged from someone's discards, and I made it work. It stood next to my bed. Half the night I would turn the knob looking for remote broadcasts from hotels and dance halls. If I could pick up Tommy Dorsey, for instance, I would listen to interminable minutes of rinky-tink in the hope of a chorus or two by Berigan (Bunny, alas). In fact, that radio was a godsend, as radios must have been to millions of lonely adolescents in those shabby years. I was crazy for two things: radical politics, fed by a scanty "underground" of students and teachers and also, strangely enough, by our little public library's quite good collection of nineteenth-century socialistic and anarchistic literature, and then music with a beat and with some relationship, however tenuous or in some cases imagined, to the blues.

This latter was fed by the radio. I remember, for instance, a dramatization of Dorothy Baker's *Young Man with a Horn*. I have no idea who the actors were or whether it was a good dramatization, but the "incidental music," for which the director had made generous allowance, was by fine musicians, including some whom I had heard at Nick's. Bobby Hackett played the cornet solos, exactly right for Dorothy Baker's forlorn hero. I squirmed and wept, with my ear pressed close to the loudspeaker, the volume turned low. My mother, who loved other kinds of music, disapproved of jazz, and although she never made an issue of it, the knowledge of her disapproval was enough. I kept my fascination to myself. Of course I had friends, though a very few, who shared my love of jazz, and one who even had a Victrola. I remember how we memorized Lester Young's solo on "Lady Be Good" (1936) and how we taught somebody's nine-year-old brother to stand on a table and sing Jimmy Lunceford's arrangement of "Margie" with what would now be called appropriate body language.

One of the reasons Dorothy Baker's novel was a good one, and I believe still is, was its remarkable faithfulness in conveying the romantic but hard-bitten idealism we felt in jazz at that time. We all knew how Leon Rappolo had gone crazy and thrown his clarinet into Lake Pontchartrain, how Boyce Brown had sacrificed his alto sax on an improvised altar and joined a monastery, how Bix Beiderbecke had drunk himself to death at the age of thirty-two; the number of such cases was great. And we understood them exactly. In our own bodies we felt the hopelessness. Jazz was the whole misery of the human species. Not an "expression" of it in the ordinary sense; I am not talking about sentiment. Jazz *was* the misery, and just as much when it was up-tempo and exuberant as when it was slow and draggy. But no horn could ever play it. Reaching for that special ultimate blue note, Bix failed again and again, and had to fail; and although his music, the concrete notes and tones, prickled our skin and wrenched our souls, we knew he had to fail. It was a myth, of course, or at least in part it was, but a myth alive in our own senses, a myth alive in the cultural reality of that time; and I don't refer only to the responses of adolescents in those depressed years either, because I heard older people speaking in the same terms. Gradually the myth has died, though it lingered a long time. Jazz has become steadily more intellectual, and musicians have become a good deal healthier. Today, in fact, the sacral sign of devotion is precisely abstinence from booze and drugs, though certain stalwarts, like Sid Catlett and Billy Taylor, knew this a long time ago.

And it does seem a long time ago, that myth by which so many of us lived. I am entering old age now, and most of the musicians I have loved the best are dead. But I am lucky, very fortunate indeed, to have known the jazz myth in its liveliest manifestations. It has been the dominant influence on my life and work down to this present moment.

Russell died in 1969. In the years before 1942 I went to hear him as often as I could, usually at Nick's. That doesn't mean I heard him often, however. I hadn't the means. Gradually I began to acquire his records, the sessions on Commodore ("Balling the Jack," "Back in Your Own Backyard"), the earlier Deccas or Bluebirds from Chicago days, others on stray labels whose names I've forgotten. Once, I remember, the director of the student union at Chapel Hill, where I was a student, gave me fifty dollars to buy records in New York for the union's collection. Fifty dollars seemed like a fortune then. I spent it at the Commodore shop on 42nd Street, and took a treasure of Commodores and Blue Notes back to Chapel Hill, including the big two-record, twelve-inch recording of "A Good Man Is Hard to Find" with Russell's remarkable opening chorus that I hadn't been able to buy for myself. After the war I lived in Chicago, where I listened to jazz of all kinds regularly, and bought many records, including numbers of secondhand records from the warehouse-like shops along Wabash Avenue. In those days jukeboxes could play only one side of a record. Often you could pick up for a dime a record utterly worn on one side, but in mint condition on the other, and sometimes the mint side, from the standpoint of jazz, was the better. The last time I saw Russell was in Chicago in about 1950. He was in woeful collapse, emaciated, so drunk he could scarcely stand, his face pallid and blurry. It was the only time I heard him play badly. It seemed as if he couldn't play more than four or five notes in a twelve-bar chorus of blues, yet I remember thinking that even so he made those four or five notes interesting. Not long after, he entered a hospital in California where the doctors managed to bring him back almost literally from the grave. He stayed nine months, but began drinking again when he was let out. At about that same time I also was hospitalized for somewhat the same reasons, i.e., in both cases the alcoholism was complicated by other ailments. I stayed nearly a year and a half, and have never taken a drink since then. Whatever romantic notions I may have had about art and alcoholism, or art and neurosis, were knocked out of me by my own experience, also by what I saw abundantly among my friends, and no one can tell me that Russell wouldn't have played better if he had been sober or at least in reasonable control. He wasn't. He was a lifelong chronic and acute alcoholic beginning in adolescence. Beyond that, I don't know much about his life, and I don't want to. Biography is a bore.

That Russell, in spite of his troubles, was truly great, that he left enough of his greatness on recordings to prove it, these are the important points. Even in the 1930s I knew he was the best of the "downtown" musicians, though I liked many of the others. And such labels weren't conspicuous then anyway, in those days before the odious term "Dixieland," in its pedantry and archaism, was applied to jazz. I recall one night, for instance, when Chu Berry, the tenor player, dropped into Nick's. Because there wasn't room for his bulk on the stand, he sat on what seemed a tiny chair on the floor next to the stand, and played thirty or forty choruses of medium-tempo blues with the other musicians, including Russell, chiming and riffing behind him. A pity it wasn't recorded. I recall another night when I talked to Russell for half an hour between sets. I write "talked to" advisedly because I had to do almost all the talking, which I wouldn't have been up to if I hadn't been boozed. Russell was mostly absent. It wasn't because he was bored or because he thought I was a square, the term used then for people who professed enthusiasm for jazz and who yelled and whistled at every drum solo, even the worst—and I heard drummers who purposely played inane Mickey Mouse licks just to watch the squares making fools of themselves—but who had no *musical* sense of what jazz was doing. I liked to think that Russell in his withdrawnness was wandering among ineffable, celestial harmonies, and perhaps he was. The possibility must not be discounted. But perhaps also he was wondering when he could pick up his laundry or how many more drinks he could hold without falling off the stand. Or he may have been brooding—and my own life as an artist leads me to think this the most likely—about the "practical" aspects of his work, how to slip in a more complex modulation at the end of the bridge in "Rocking Chair," how to define further his own relationship to the rest of jazz.

Russell did not come from Chicago, and liked to deny, especially in his later years, that he had anything to do with Chicago jazz. On the contrary, he said, he had worked for such a long time at Nick's, with other musicians known for their general derivation from the jazz played by young white Chicagoans during the late 1920s and early 1930s, only because the contingencies of life had pushed him into it. Maybe so. Maybe also, as he said, he learned a great deal from listening when he was a young man to clarinetists from New Orleans, Jimmie Noone especially, but also Johnny Dodds, Darnell Howard, Omer Simeon, etc. No doubt this is true, and Noone's influence especially can be heard in the work of other Chicagoans, such as Benny Goodman, Rod Cless, etc. But it is clear to me, and I believe to many others, that Russell's own style derives primarily from Frank Teschemacher, the clarinetist who was born in Chicago, who died in 1932 at the age of twenty-five,

and whose reedy, squealing, derisive tone Russell's so nearly resembles. (Russell could easily have heard Teschemacher by 1925,
or perhaps as early as 1922.) It is also clear to me that Russell's
characteristic rhythmic and melodic figures are not those of the
musicians from New Orleans, but are much more closely allied to
northern and white usage, especially to the work of cornet players
like Beiderbecke, McPartland, Nichols, Berigan, etc. I mean his
manner of skipping irregularly among the beats, his held notes in
the upper register, his abrupt changes of register, his fierce attack, and his avoidance of the legato runs and flourishes so essential to the style of southern black reed players.

Though it has been said so often that it seems meaningless, I
still think it important to emphasize that between the great years
of Louis Armstrong, 1926–28, and the emergence of the western
or Kansas City style a decade later, the primary influence on American jazz was Beiderbecke. (By influence I mean less the work of
these musicians themselves, since all were playing in their characteristic modes before the dates in question, Armstrong as early
as 1920–21, Beiderbecke in 1924–25, than their styles as they
emerged in the work of other musicians.) This means a good deal
more than the mere impress of Beiderbecke's personal mannerisms. It means that for those few years jazz was a brass music, not
a reed music, as it had been before and would be after. This may
seem strange at first; it certainly will to those who have not listened closely. But what Armstrong contributed to the development of the jazz cornet was what he imitated, or tried to imitate,
from the lyricism of the southern clarinetists of his own generation. Why did he choose to do this? In part, I think, because the
reed players were better trained than most other black musicians
in New Orleans of the period from 1910 to 1925. Also in part because the clarinetists could get closer than the brass players, in
both timbre and flexibility, to the vocal blues tradition, which was
still dominant in the consciousness of southern black musicians
of the 1920s. (Years later Mutt Carey remarked to me that "the
trumpet is a lousy instrument.") The result, though it seems a
paradox, is that the black Armstrong played his cornet (later his
trumpet) like a clarinet, and the white Russell, who was a crucial
six years younger, played his clarinet like a cornet, imitating
Beiderbecke indirectly. Only in the late 1930s did the reed style
become dominant again with younger black musicians from various parts of the country but especially from west of the Mississippi, Lester Young, Ben Webster, Johnny Hodges, Pete Brown,

and hundreds of others. The case of Coleman Hawkins, who developed on his own, or nearly, and who lived in Europe during many of the years I am writing about, is more difficult. Yet I hear an affinity between Hawkins and Russell, although I don't remember any writer or musician who has pointed it out. Other reed players of Russell's generation who used a cornet-like tone and attack were Bud Freeman, Boyce Brown, Benny Goodman (though Goodman's playing changed considerably when he began acquiring a "classical" technique), Eddie Miller, and others, all of whom were Chicagoans, and some of whom, especially Freeman, may have influenced the later "rough" style of tenormen like Illinois Jacquet and Eddie Davis.

I suppose I must add, though I should think everyone must know it, that the chief influence on Beiderbecke was Armstrong. And one of the chief influences on Lester Young and Ben Webster was Frank Trumbauer, who played with Beiderbecke but took his own manner more from southern reed players like Noone, Bigard, and Bechet (and from his own classical training) than from Armstrong. Well, the genealogy of cyclic manners, as opposed to individual styles, is fascinating, especially in jazz, so much of which, even from the early period, is on records; but finally its complexity is too great to permit more than rudimentary conjecture.

Russell's best work, at least on records, was done after the doctors had patched him together. In the middle and late 1950s he was given more opportunity than he had had earlier to play with small groups in the mainstream tradition of that time, the four-beat, loosely swinging jazz that had been dominant since about 1938. If I were asked to choose one phrase that shows Russell at his best, though of course it can't be done, I would say the second eight bars of "Lulu's Back in Town" on an album Russell cut with Buck Clayton and a rhythm section at some time around 1960 (Prestige, SVLP 2008, n.d.). In the first eight bars Clayton states the theme with his trumpet, this tritest of trite themes, with very little melodic variation but with enough rhythmic variation to establish the group's collective authority and get the performance off to a good start. Then Russell enters. He enters not with a restatement, not with a variation, not with a noodling improvisation on the chord structure, but with a totally new and forever surprising counter-statement; in effect, a new melody both more interesting and far more vigorous than the original, although it retains a recognizable resemblance to the original. It is of the same genre as the "Variations on a Theme by Haydn" of Brahms, and like that work is an assertion of creative independence made stronger, not weaker, by its relationship to the prior text.

This was Russell's greatness from the beginning. In all art there is a powerful element of backward reference, as we know. Among the Chicago-oriented jazz musicians who worked at Nick's and similar establishments from 1935 on into the 1960s, this was a primary concern. In the work of Wild Bill Davison, for instance, one hears the whole white evolution of the jazz cornet: Beiderbecke, Nichols, McPartland, Spanier, Butterfield, and scores of others. It is a summation. Nothing at all wrong with this, of course; the tradition is powerful because it is good, alive, and supportive—I mean among the real jazz musicians, not the "Dixielanders." When Max Kaminsky repeated, twenty years later, King Oliver's improvisation in "Dippermouth Blues," adding only enough of his own spontaneous feeling to dispel any notion of contrived imitativeness, listeners were delighted. Recognition is always a positive, if secondary, esthetic effect. Nor was it limited to that era only (hundreds, probably thousands of musicians today are trying to absorb, integrate, and re-express the greatness of John Coltrane) or of that medium (what Pope did with the closed couplet would be poetically meaningless without the backward reference to Dryden, Waller, Donne, and Jonson).

Nevertheless the truly great artist brings to the tradition something personal and original, something larger than a mere augmentation of previously known inflections and textures, something new. This seems inescapable. Pope did it in his later work (the fourth book of the second *Dunciad*, the "Epistle to Dr. Arbuthnot," etc.), and Russell did it in all his best work after, say, 1934. In a musical environment heavily reliant on the tradition, he stood out as the individualist, the originator. His improvisations were always surprising, full of unexpected notes, tones, and changes. He was continually reaching for the further range of musical expressiveness and his own imagination. Considerably before the harmonic explosion of the bop movement in the late 1940s, Russell was experimenting with extended chords and unusual harmonies. Naturally he imitated himself and fell into habits, i.e., characteristic melodic figures and shapes. All jazz musicians must do this, not only because they normally work so much that no amount of inventiveness could sustain a continually new line of improvisation, but also because self-imitation is one of the instinctual devices that the improvising imagination uses in order to control and limit itself. This is very evident in the work of

Charlie Parker, for instance, who nevertheless was probably the greatest innovator we have known in jazz. One could always recognize a passage by Russell instantly, I believe, from its melodic qualities alone, i.e., if somehow it were played by another musician whose tone and technique were perfectly conventional. He repeatedly used a dozen or more improvisational concepts that were unique with him, such as the very quiet, staccato choruses in the chalumeau, the screeching high note, the sequence of arhythmic notes neither on nor off the beat, the tricky descent by grace notes from the upper to lower register, the reaching up at the end of a passage to a note farther out on the dominant chord progression than one would expect, and so on. Beyond this, of course, Russell's tone and dynamic technique were far from conventional; they were highly personal and fully assimilated to his melodic sensibility. His work was as self-contained as that of any artist I can think of in any medium. For this reason, he was not a modernist. When he tried to work with musicians or materials associated with the line of development from Parker and Monk and Davis to Rollins and Coltrane, he often conspicuously failed. He had already become fully himself in his music before these later musicians arrived, though some of what he had done, especially harmonically, prefigured their ideas, as they themselves acknowledged. Beyond this, I suspect Russell did not greatly care about anyone's music but his own. He listened to himself. Like all great artists, he was at his best among others who were strong, gifted, reliable, but fundamentally unassertive; that is, supportive but never competitive. Perhaps this is why Russell did some of his best work with musicians like George Wettling (who was not at all the two-beat, bump-and-grind drummer that many have taken him for), Jimmy Giuffre, and Buck Clayton, as different as all these were from one another. At the same time one must add that Russell was so highly respected among the best musicians of his time that even the thumping egos, men like Coleman Hawkins, were glad to praise him and work with him.

Russell's individuality was almost unfailing. Every melody came to him as if out of the blue. A good example is "Exactly Like You," a standard pop tune used by hundreds of musicians, yet always with a certain sameness in their melodic insights, no matter if the musician were Bunny Berigan, Lionel Hampton, or Thelonious Monk; it was a tune that had become virtually encrusted with convention. Yet when Russell recorded it in 1958 (reissued in 1982 on Xanadu, 192), he approached it as no one had before, as if he had never heard it until that day, and broke it into phrasings, both melodic and rhythmic, that were entirely his own. At the same time he could play a straight sweet ballad with only the slightest variations, as he did with "Over the Rainbow," and evoke from it by intensity of musical concentration, as evidenced in timbre and attack, a beauty that one would have said the song did not contain.

Someone once remarked that Russell was the greatest poet after Yeats. A ludicrous statement, one feels. Yet I'm glad it was made, because it points in the direction of something that I think I have come to see after a life of thinking about the art of my time. The great contribution of the twentieth century to art is the idea of spontaneous improvisation within a determined style, a style comprising equally or inseparably both conventional and personal elements. What does this mean? It means a great deal more than the breakup of traditional prosody or rules of composition, as announced in 1910 by Ezra Pound and Pablo Picasso. It means the final abandonment of the neo-classical idea of structure as a function of form, which the romantics and postromantics of the nineteenth century had never given up. Instead structure has become a function of feeling.

Take the simplest structural problem of all: what is the right length for a poem? In the past this was determined either by fixed external forms, such as the sonnet or ballade, or by extrinsic notions of unity, narrative verisimilitude, lyrical or argumentative consistency, and other such fundamentally architectonic considerations. Today the open-ended, random, improvised, indeterminate poem, whatever its length, concluding usually with inconclusion, is our norm. And the transition may be seen with extraordinary clarity in the work of Yeats. Beginning with some of his middle poems, such as "The Cold Heaven," "The Magi," "The Wild Swans at Coole," "In Memory of Alfred Pollexfen," and continuing to late poems like the Crazy Jane sequence, "Lapis Lazuli," "The Three Bushes," "Under Ben Bulben," etc., the poet evolves a flexible, personal style that permits him to extemporize (no matter how he revised and even if in fact he put his poems through many revisions, just as jazz musicians put their improvisations through many remembered versions) within very simple formal limits, as simple, for instance, as the twelve-bar form of the conventional blues. The endings obviously come where passion has expended itself, not where passion has been crimped to fit a premeditated structure. I know, one can call forth somewhat similar poems from the past, e.g., Elizabethan sonnet sequences,

"The Prelude," "In Memoriam." I know, too, that our century in art has been dominated by extreme formalism, formalism for its own sake, at certain times and places, especially in composed music and the visual arts. But I am speaking of tendencies, of attitudes so large that we can scarcely find ourselves in them. And these are important.

Certainly the feeling of a good late poem by Yeats, the way it buds itself and burgeons in our receptive imaginations, is different from the feeling of any poetry in the past. Perhaps it approaches the preclassical informalism of Gilgamesh, Greek pastoral, or the Border Ballads, as Russell's improvisations in some sense approach Arabic folk music. But in both instances the modern artist is a sophisticated individual, not an anonymous collective, and this makes an enormous difference. The individual, recognized by style, which in turn is a function partly of convention and back-reference but more significantly of personality, is the master artist of our time; not a romantic ego or a thumping ideologue, but a genius in and of humility, such as I feel both Yeats and Russell at their best exemplify. It would be silly to say that jazz had a direct influence on Yeats or on any other particular artist of our century. Yet I believe there is a connection. I believe it probably springs from prior complexities of cultural evolution too obscure for us to see with clarity. But improvisation is the mode, as independence and freedom are the conditions, of great art in our time.

I believe further that jazz offers the critic and esthetician an especially rich body of material upon which to work, if only because its development has been so rapid and its history so well recorded. I have thought this for forty years, but I never found a way to proceed. Technical criticism can be moderately helpful, and I hope that some trained critic will eventually notate and explicate Russell's music for us, as Gunther Schuller has done for Armstrong. But the usefulness of such criticism is very limited, first, because so few readers are trained to read a score, and secondly, because no system of notation we now have can convey all the significant qualities of a jazz improvisation. Should we distribute a cassette tape with each critical essay? That would be infeasible; but at the same time the best jazz criticism I have encountered in my lifetime, though still extremely rare, has been on the radio. This is something for young critics to ponder. What I know for a fact is that the kind of impressionistic writing about jazz that has been foisted on us in superabundance during the past three or four decades is utterly useless; the kind of thing done by Whitney Balliett, John Williams, and sometimes Nat Hentoff. It exploits the musicians as romantic, not to say psychoneurotic, personalities, and it exploits the reader by promising what it cannot deliver, an explanation or at least a description of the expressiveness of jazz, which every fully engaged listener longs for.

What does jazz express? Some people do not like chocolate ice cream, which is something I know but do not understand (using these terms in their Schopenhauerean refinement and extension). In the same way I know that many people do not respond to jazz, are unaware of its expressiveness, but I do not understand it. In this the analogy with poetry is exact; fully half or more of the students in my graduate workshops cannot hear poetry as concrete verbal structures of sound and rhythm, whether the poetry be old or new; by miseducation, by genetic derangement, by God knows what horrendous carcinomas of the sensibility engendered by our social, historical, and cultural pollution, they have been rendered deaf to the powers and beauties of spoken vocalizations. As a teacher, I cannot deal with them, although they move me to extremes of apprehension and sympathy. I believe, then, that the values and feelings expressed in poetry are poetic; they are not in the substance of the poem, they are not even in the language or the figures of the poem, but they float above the poem, a continuum of imaginative and affective abstraction. The poem is only a thing, an instance. Yet the values and feelings, as they evolve in the reader's mind, are inextricably bound to the concrete instance. In just this way the values and feelings expressed in jazz are bound to the concrete music, the *sounds,* yet they float above it, and they certainly have nothing to do with song lyrics, titles, or any literary or literal signifiers whatsoever. Moreover, they have nothing to do with any cultural adherences or extrapolations whatsoever. We know that jazz was engendered among suffering black people at a certain time and in a certain place. Presumably this knowledge is effectively undetachable from the music. But it is not in or of the *music,* the concrete notes and tones, and if the *music* came to us from another planet, picked up and recorded by our radio astronomers, it would evoke in us the same *musical* responses. In other words, the whole spectrum of human affect as aroused by interaction between the existent and existence—fear, hate, love, pride, humiliation, etc.—is irrelevant. This is what I meant when I wrote earlier that jazz *is* misery. I was being precise; misery is feeling and value, but it is not emotion; it is the experience of immediate sensory apprehension and simultaneous mental comprehension. It may or may not consequently give rise to emotion properly so called. Jazz as misery exists either in irrelation to ideas or in relations too tenuous and uncategorical to know, I'm not sure which. And this is the same as saying that esthetic expressiveness in general is unknowable though understandable, intuitively realizable on *a priori* grounds. Then what is the difference between emotion and feeling? Emotion is a state of mind or, if you like, a state of spirit; its function in consciousness is cognitive. Feeling, as the term implies, is a state of the senses, a somatic reverberation; its function in consciousness is intuitive. And a very good place to look for and study feeling is in jazz.

Have I found a way to write about it? In the past I have used jazz imaginatively as a focus of experience in my poems, and I have written a few pieces of tangential prose—book reviews, essays in which jazz appears only exemplificatively. Here, in this piece that is part memoir, part appreciation, and part conjecture, I have tried to begin to attack the central problem of jazz, which is the central problem of art, head on. Once I wrote a poem called "The Joy and Agony of Improvisation." People ask me what the title means, since it seems to have nothing to do with the content of the poem. It doesn't; it refers to the *making* of the poem: improvisation was the mode, joy and agony were what I felt while improvising. But they were not joy and agony as these words are used in ordinary human affairs. They were something else altogether; in the vocabulary of esthetic expressiveness they might just as well be called X and Y. I feel some readers—poets and musicians—will intuit the quality of X and Y, and hence will understand what they do not know. For them the title of the poem will be justified. But I want the problem explained; I want to know as well as understand. I am not content to rest in mystery, though I recognize that many people are and that they not only accept but seek their existence in the unknowable. I am too much an up-country Yankee pragmatist for that. I think some of us are concerned for the differences and similarities between value and meaning, not only in jazz and poetry but perhaps in political belief; we are concerned for the relationships among them, concerned for esthetic consciousness in society and individuals; and we, I believe, must concentrate our intelligence and intuition on the problem of functional expressiveness.

Meanwhile, how sadly the art of improvisation has declined since the work of Yeats and Russell. I don't say we haven't had many another great *improvvisatore*. We have. And obviously jazz is better off today than poetry. But the falling off in all sectors is evident. In poetry we have improvisation by the yard, the furlong, but no style, no passion, and hence no structure. Our workshops are rote-drills in formulas and artifice. In jazz we have much *interesting* music, among both the élitist conceptualizers, many of whom have become significantly attached to the academy, and some younger musicians (Scott Hamilton, Warren Vaché) who have gone back to pick up the unfinished themalities of mainstream jazz in the 1940s and 1950s. But greatness, at least for the time being, seems to have gone. All the more reason to pay attention—critically and objectively, yes, but especially subjectively, for the subject *is* our understanding—to the achieved greatness we already possess on vinyl and paper. More and more I see how effectual is the brooding, loving assessment that goes on inside our heads all our lives, the muddle of shifting affections, something permitted us far more than to most people in the past by the fact of our being able to read and listen cheaply and at home, and how right and useful this is in our appreciation of the masters and in sustaining the genuineness of our own sensibilities— imagine! in our own living rooms we can hear all ten of Mahler's symphonies in succession, which he himself could never do, since reading a score is not the same and can never be the same as hearing with our bodies, our whole bodies. At the same time we see over and over again how attempts to invent or impose objective rankings lead only to error, to *mis-con-cep-tus*. God, where is our old America that abhorred the doctrinaire! Do I leap too swift for you, inchling? Well, for forty years of my own brooding I have wavered often as this or that power of soul, heart, and intellect has seized me; yet again and again I have come back to my understanding that William Butler Yeats and Charles Ellsworth Russell have given me more esthetic pleasure, if only an iota more, than any other artists of this century. I may waver again. No matter. The point is understanding, which is all that can save human beings from dying in error.

PARAGRAPH

Oh I loved you Pete Brown. And you were a brother
to me Joe Marsala. And you too sweet Billy Kyle.
You Sid Bechet. And Benny Carter.
And Jo Jones. Cozy Cole.
Cootie Williams. Dickie Wells. Al Hall. Ben Webster.
Matty Matlock. Lou McGarity. Mel Powell. Fats Waller.
Freddie Green. Rex Stewart. Wilbur & Sid
de Paris. Russ Procope. And Sister Ida
Cox dont forget her. And Omer Simeon. Joe Smith.
Zutty Singleton. Charlie Shavers.
Specs Powell. Red Norvo. Vic Dickenson. J.C.
   Higginbotham.
Nappy Lamare. Earl Hines. Buck Clayton.
Roy Eldridge. Pops Foster. Johnny Hodges. Ed Hall.
Art Tatum. Frankie Newton. Chu Berry. Billy Taylor.
And oh incomparable James P. Johnson.

                    Brothers I loved you all.

GOT THOSE
FOREVER INADEQUATE BLUES

The origin of the blues will never be known precisely. But in recent years musicologists have made great strides, with the consequence that now, owing partly to the relative abundance of
recorded evidence, we know more about the beginning of the
blues than we know about the beginning of any other major folk
art. What do we know?

1. The blues did not emerge gradually, as earlier investigators
conjectured, but instead were a quite abrupt development that
probably occurred between 1895 and 1900.

2. The place cannot be determined, and in any event one must
allow for the possibility, some say the probability, that the blues as
a distinct form—the three-line, twelve-bar strophe—came into
being at several places simultaneously. But the region is clear
enough: the central part of the deep south, Mississippi, Louisiana, eastern Texas, and eastern Arkansas.

3. Musically speaking, the blues derived immediately from Afroamerican folk sources, especially spirituals, field chants and hollers, and what were called "jump-ups," songs with two-line stanzas
that may survive in such eight-bar blues as "How Long" and
"Cherry Red." The only white contribution was to some of the
words of the blues, which show an affinity with Angloamerican
folk themes from the mountainous areas of northern Mississippi
and southern Tennessee. I should make it clear, however, that I
am concerned only with the music here, not with the poetry or
what musicians call the "lyrics." Nor am I concerned with rags,
marches, show tunes, opera, or any of the other musical forms in
which blacks and whites both participated and which, together
with the blues, entered into the evolution of jazz.

4. The primary or germinal derivation of the blues is from the
traditional music of West Africa, which can be traced with reason-

able assurance to the seventeenth century or earlier, and particularly from two elements of that music, namely, its polyrhythmic beat and its microtonality, although both these elements were considerably attenuated in America.

Indeed, what else should we expect? The slaves brought their music with them, a complex, distinctive, and very expressive music; but like all radically displaced people in history, they lost touch with their cultural origins, partly through "normal" dissociation, partly because their whole heritage, religious and cultural, was intentionally suppressed by the slaveowners. (Drumming, for instance, was forbidden on the grounds, not entirely unlikely, that it was used by blacks to communicate from one plantation to another and therefore was a means to foment rebellion.) Thus although we can hear polyrhythmic elements in spirituals, hollers, and other black music deriving from slavery, as heard in the field recordings made by Alan Lomax in the 1930s, and although a polyrhythmic tendency is discernible in the recorded instrumental work of early blues musicians, especially guitarists, this important aspect of black musical consciousness is greatly simplified in comparison to the extraordinary recorded performances of West African drumming. As the years passed, Afroamerican music, including the blues, became more and more fixed on a plain 4/4 measure, no matter how the beats were accented. The polyrhythmic tradition, the *feeling*, was gone, or at least much weakened. In fact very talented drummers in recent decades, like Max Roach and Shelly Manne, have had to relearn the concepts of polyrhythmic figuration partly by listening to "ethnological" recordings from Africa.

By polyrhythm I mean the imposition of different meters upon one another in a controlled, significant, and apprehensible pattern, a kind of layering that reaches almost inconceivable complexity—at least to Euroamerican senses—among the multi-percussive ensembles of Africa.

When it comes to the melodic element of the blues, which is what primarily concerns me here, the case is both more complicated and more interesting. In African music one can hear melodic figures of three distinct pitches within one semi-tone. This is true of both vocal and instrumental performances. I emphasize that this microtonality is pure and natural, however sophisticated; it is the intrinsic factor of African musical expressiveness. But in America it ran head on into the European diatonic scale and into European instruments tuned to the diatonic scale. In other words, African musical sensibility could not function in its pure essentiality within the European modes of the musical environment it encountered in America, nor could it adapt itself, again purely, to the mechanical gradations of frequencies built into most European musical instruments. The conventional European system of notation was, and is, entirely inadequate.[1]

The result was a forced compromise, that is, the "blues scale," as it has often been called. The European diatonic scale could not be adapted to African microtonal feeling without hesitations or a kind of indeterminacy, usually on the third, fifth, and seventh notes. Thus in F-major, the third note could be either A or A-flat, the fifth note either C or C-flat, the seventh either E or E-flat. But this meant a loss of purity; the African pitch would have been neither flatted nor natural, but something in between. Purity was lost, and before long it was forgotten—at least on the level of conscious musicality—and in its place came a bending, slurring, and wavering of pitch that is the primary melodic quality of the blues. And this, I believe, is what accounts, musically, for the expressiveness of the blues.

What I mean is this: if for purposes of analysis we leave aside all questions of cultural adherence, all questions of literary and poetic effects (both verbal and nonverbal), all questions of texture, timbre, tempo, and rhythmic interplay, and if we consider the blues as purely musical sound (in the sense that this can be said of a Bach chaconne), then this blues note, the blurred third, fifth, and seventh, is what makes the music esthetically (sensually) effectual for those who can hear it—not everyone, by any means— with the same sensitivity to blues sound that is evident in those who perform it.

The blues were invented *by* blacks *in* America. My italicized prepositions are equally important. The blues were probably invented and were certainly developed by blacks whose musical sensibilities had been assimilated to the European diatonic mode, however much or little of African feeling for microtonal purity may have lingered in their subconscious or semiconscious musical imaginations. And of course the white musicians who contributed to the blues—relatively few in number, but they have their importance—were equipped with diatonic musical feeling from their beginnings, whether or not they had formal training: it is the whole western context of music. Consequently the blues were a mode in conflict with itself, a microtonal pitch seeking and failing to find its place in a diatonic scale. The blues could not have happened without Africa. Equally they could not have happened without Europe.

The blues are a seeking and a failure. And they are perpetual: both musically and in all other ways, the blues have no resolution. The final chord may be the dominant, but it does not yield a musical conclusion precisely because the dominant (the fifth) is a blues pitch, slurred and uncertain, and often blues players actually end with a diminished chord: the sound goes silent but it never ends. If I try to describe the effect of blues in words, I find over and over again that I cannot. If I say, for example, that the blues note induces a sense of twisting or wrenching, this connotes physical pain, but although a kind of pain is involved, it is not like a headache or a broken arm. If I say that the blues note is orgasmic, this implies sexuality, but although an analogy exists between the sensuality of sex and the sensuality of blues, again it is not the same. And so on. I could go through the whole emotive vocabulary, as people often do, saying "joy," "sorrow," "agony," etc., and never arrive at a linguistic formulation of the musical expressiveness of the blues. The best I have been able to do so far is to say that it is a sensual experience of seeking and failing, that is, of inadequacy.

Again, if I say that the blues are the musical expression of existentialist thought and feeling, or even if I say that the experience of the blues is consonant with the experience of existentialist thought and feeling, I am obviously overstepping the bounds of historical license. I cannot prove it; neither can anyone else. Yet I believe this is an aspect of the truth of our time. Quite aside from the immense cultural place occupied by Afroamerican music itself in our civilization, its reverberations elsewhere are perhaps a kind of proof. The songs of Kurt Weill and Bertolt Brecht are neither blues nor jazz; but Weill's music, in its totally different environment, nevertheless has some demonstrable affinities with Afroamerican music, and not many people would deny a direct influence. The combination of those blues-like melodies with Brecht's sardonic verses makes a reflection of what we call German expressionist feeling in the 1920s that is remarkably acute; and it is without doubt existentialist. Only this can account for the continuing popularity of songs composed so long before our present monstrous life began. (Nostalgia is not enough.) The same can be said of Gershwin's compositions, especially *Porgy and Bess,* which remains our best and certainly our best-known American opera. What a sham it is in many ways!—an opera about black life composed and written by two white men. But Gershwin was musically a man with a little black in him, as more and more Americans of every color have become; and not only Americans but people all over the world. (Yet an exception seems to exist—paradoxically, not to say oppositively—among Africans in Africa. They have not been able to play Afroamerican music with real insight, at least up until recently. I think the reason is that they know the purity of their own microtonality too well, so that the blues seem to them only a debasement.) Gershwin caught enough of the blues mode in his own melodies to make them genuinely expressive as para-blues. The analogy with other composers of the past who incorporated folk motifs in their work is too well known to need more than mentioning.[2]

The blues became, of course, the principal element of jazz. In the 1920s and 1930s, when jazz developed so rapidly, the blues mode became dominant in the performance of all the music adapted by jazz musicians to their purposes, and the slurred thirds, fifths, and sevenths (the seeking and failing) characterized jazz improvisation on even the trashiest themes from Tin Pan Alley, which had been composed squarely in the diatonic tradition. (The singing of pop "ballads" by Billie Holiday shows this very clearly, as does the playing of Lester Young, Buck Clayton, and the others who backed her, including Teddy Wilson, though the question of how the blues scale is played on the piano would require a long digression. But thousands and thousands of musicians in that period were doing the same thing.) I don't mean to say that jazz is not complex, a music of many strands; but the blues were one of its primary impulses, and remained so for a long time. More recently, it seems to me, the element of blues has receded in jazz. The musicians have again and again surpassed themselves in technique, until now we are quite accustomed to hearing passages on the tenor sax, for instance, that would have been thought impossible by musicians of the early period. But the saxophone is a diatonic instrument (though easy to adapt to a slurred pitch), and today's jazz musicians, many of them trained in the conservatory, have more and more moved away from the blues scale. To my mind the line of development in jazz that includes Charlie Parker, Miles Davis, Sonny Rollins, and John Coltrane, brilliant innovative musicians without any doubt, has nevertheless tended to lose one of the truly distinctive ingredients of Afroamerican music. Once a few years ago I remarked to a very literate black scholar that Coltrane was doing in jazz what Bartók had done in European music. "Yes," he said. "But Trane does it with soul." Well, if soul means blues, as it does for me and as it at least once did for the vast majority of black Americans, then Coltrane, in spite of his truly marvelous inventions, tended to depart from one important Afroamerican source. He did not play in the blues scale, especially toward the end of his life.

He did other things, however, that were in fact expressive of essential inadequacy, and I know that many arguments could be brought against my view. Furthermore there are plenty of modernist jazz musicians who have expressly extrapolated their ideas from the convention of the blues, Thelonious Monk, Ornette Coleman, Charlie Mingus, Rahsaan Roland Kirk, and many others. (Dollar Brand, the remarkable South African pianist, is a somewhat special case, whose work requires far more attention than I can give it here. I think he is musically neither African nor Afroamerican, as I am using these terms in this essay.) But let me go back to what I know more about. When Leon Rappolo, the white clarinetist from New Orleans in the very early days, walked out to the end of a pier and threw his horn as far as he could into Lake Pontchartrain, and when he was then hauled off to spend the rest of his life in a psychiatric institution, no doubt he was certifiably deranged and something of the sort would have happened to him anyway, whether he was a musician or not. But he was a musician, a jazz musician, and his action became a symbolic one for a great many of the rest of us. How often when I was young did I hear musicians groan or sigh and then say: "This goddamn thing just won't play what I hear in my head." It was true. And it was not simply a question of their limited technique, because the further truth was that even what they heard in their heads was unhearable: the seeking and failing. It was a continual *crise d'esprit*. To some of the best musicians an instinctive means of accommodation to this musical stress and distress came from their artistic imaginations, a means not far removed, I think, from the lucid acceptance, denial, and creative continuance suggested by Albert Camus for the survival of humanity exiled in the condition of the absurd. To others, including again some of the best, insanity, alcohol, drugs, and early death were the answer. In either case it is the blues.

NOTES

1. I am not a musicologist, but a poet. Like most artists I distrust scholarship, especially its disposition toward misplaced emphasis and narrow pedantry; yet I must rely on the work of scholars. Much of what I have written so far here, though it can be found in many sources, has been taken from *Deep Blues*, by Robert Palmer (New York, 1981), which is a readable, brief account. But I must add that Palmer's concentration on the blues of the Delta (central Mississippi and part of eastern Arkansas) results in a very distorted history; moreover, his implication throughout that musicians who could sight-read "Twinkle, Twinkle, Little Star" must be automatically disqualified from consideration is unfortunate to say the least. My own view is the opposite. Musicians like Louis Armstrong and Sidney Bechet in the 1920s extended and enhanced the blues, made them more, not less, bluesy, as did the best of their white imitators, musicians like Bix Beiderbecke and Pee Wee Russell. They did this precisely because their musical awareness, which came in part from training, permitted them to hear the more developed and more expressive chordal modulations implicit in the primitive blues of the earlier period. Meanwhile the country blues singers and musicians of the Delta, although they made considerable merely stylistic advance, added nothing harmonically or melodically to the basic concept of the blues.

2. Is the evolution and meaning of literature, especially poetry, in the twentieth century analogous to the blues? Yes. Poetry has become more and more improvisatory, unfinishable, and subjective. To reduce poetry to its sensual element alone is much more difficult than finding the blues scale in the blues; still I believe a formal searching and failing is a sensory semeiosis of our poetry. One thinks immediately of W.C. Williams and the "variable foot," then of the prosodic stretching in work by Levertov, Creeley, Duncan, and others. But essentially the same awareness of formal inadequacy is the *expressive* element in the best work of Yeats and even Frost, and indeed in all the most characteristic writing of the existentialist era. This is a point to be considered at more length elsewhere.

THE INTENTIONAL ALLIGATOR

Recently a young friend offered me a number of shirts, the kind once called polo shirts, and told me he couldn't wear them because they had the image of an alligator fixed to the left front sector. "Too preppy," he said. "Why don't you take the alligator off?" I said. "Oh, I can't be bothered," he said. Or words to that effect.

Now I have two principles that I stick to closely. One is never to buy any paper. The other is to buy as few articles of clothing as possible, usually nothing but underwear and socks. So much paper and clothing are floating around in the general environment, there for the taking, slightly used but perfectly functional, that my no doubt obsolete Yankee sense of thrift rebels at the thought of paying money for them. So I accepted the shirts. I wear them. And I think to myself, as old people do, that the young are too much influenced by their reflexive susceptibility to images, and also that they are too wasteful.

Yet I am an artist and have been all my life. And art, considered from the working artist's point of view, is based on the idea that images of all kinds can be used to elicit widely recognizable, efficacious, generally nonrational responses, and on the further idea that procedural efficiency is the last desideration in the artist's *modus operandi* and that a large factor of wasted effort is not only unavoidable but probably advisable.

The world knows, and endlessly points out, that consistency is the hobgoblin of small minds. The world also knows, but rarely any longer acknowledges—the best-kept secret being that which everyone guesses—that the human mind is a natural organ and that one of its natural functions is precisely the search for consistency, i.e., for a unified and hence more serviceable system of values. At any rate I am pestered by the very obvious inconsistency between what I approve as an artist and what I disapprove as a member of our consumerist, image-ridden society. Why? Because I am a human being with a human mind, born to be pestered.

And also because I see a direct historical development from the artistic or more broadly creative (to use a word I don't like) upsurge of the Renaissance to our own wastefulness and subverted imaginations.

This is not the place to argue my historical view. Besides, I am confident that anyone who thinks about such matters, meaning anyone who is likely to be reading these words, agrees with my interpretation, in spite of all the exceptions and provisos that must be attached to it. What is important here is to resolve the inconsistency between what I believe as an artist and what I believe as a citizen. How? The answer is easy: by making qualitative judgments. But qualitative judgment immediately projects us into relativity, the practical need to say that one thing is "better" than another of the same kind. And to find and apply a consistent method of making such relative judgments is hard, damnably hard, as the whole evolution of human thought demonstrates with utter, dismaying clarity.

Usually the search for a way to make consistently valid relative judgments has been conducted mentally—that is, by working backward in logic to basic and undisputed premises, which may then be used as criteria for judgments in the practical world. This is the way of Socrates, the philosopher's way, and it is also the way, though many of them would like to deny it, of social scientists. As a human being with a human mind, I cannot disavow it, although I can say with confidence that so far it has never worked. As an artist, however, I *must* disavow it because I know that no criteria for judgment can be valid universally or anywhere near universally; that is, none can be discovered that has a sufficiently wide application to be useful in practice. Every judgment I have encountered, every judgment I myself have been inclined to make, can be refuted simply by visiting a museum or opening an anthology. Then how does one proceed?

Let's begin with the alligator. The philosopher would say that the alligator is a spurious symbol of specious values, and he—or she—would argue backward through a sequence of propositions until some *a priori* criterion, such as human happiness or revealed truth, was reached, at which point the alligator could be shown to be logically and radically divergent. The artist cannot do this, knowing that art must be free and that prescriptions will not work. Art created in methodical accordance with prior tenets can never be new. On the contrary, it will be fixed: ultimately as repetitious, unimaginative, and hence essentially inartistic as any ritual. The imagination is the part of the mind that seeks not certainty but surprise.

The sociologist, on the other hand, would say that the alligator is symbolic of specious values because those values have been imposed rather than derived; that is, they have been invented by identifiable minds, those of the shirt manufacturers and their advertising agents, and have not been taken from the common fund of attitudes, which is the sociologist's name for universal values. Moreover, the specious values of the alligator have been violently impressed, by the kind of force that is called persuasion, on the minds of the people who acknowledge it, whether by acceptance or by rejection. The artist may agree that this is indeed the case, but he cannot question the method as a method. He knows that particular images in particular works of art, even though they may be related (as Carl Jung pointed out) to certain prior and common and therefore archetypal clusters of human feeling, nevertheless take their particular power from the imaginations of the artists who have made use of them. In this sense they, like the alligator, have been imposed, not derived. They have been imposed by exactly the same persuasive violence, which in art we call esthetic corresponsiveness, that we know is at the heart of all imaginative transactions.

Yet every artist knows that the alligator is in fact a spurious symbol for specious values. How does he know? It is not enough to say that the alligator does not excite or move him, and that therefore it is not functionally esthetic. The truth is that if he looks around at the world he will see very clearly that the alligator *is* effective, that huge numbers of people are affected by it. He may wish that his own poems or paintings could produce anything like as pervasive a response. Speaking for myself, I'd be overcome with astonished gratification. So I don't think the artist can make an argument against the alligator on the basis of any notion of efficacy. It won't work. What else is left? The philosophical method (reason), the sociological method (empiricism), and the artistic method (esthetic efficacy) are all denied to the artist, though this does not mean they aren't still useful in general.

What remains is the human method. I call it this, not in an exclusionary sense, but simply because it seems to me more human than any of the others. It is the awareness of will. Schopenhauer said that the awareness of Will, which he liked to capitalize, is the one awareness that precedes all others in our consciousness. What we want is what we know best, in other words. I'm inclined to agree. And in respect to art and the imagination, it seems to me that what we are aware of before anything else is the aspect of Will called intention.

Awareness of intention is more human than other mental awarenesses because it is, as we say, intuitive. Schopenhauer said that it comes from understanding, as opposed to knowing and reasoning; a common enough observation. We cannot analyze our acts of intuition because we lack, so far, the means to distinguish the constituent actions that go into them, or even, if we could distinguish them, to measure them. Yet I believe we do intuitively recognize the intentions of nearly all works of art, to say nothing of human acts in general. Indeed, by virtue of the shape it takes to become a work of art, the work must announce its intention; it has no choice. The shape, considered functionally, is the intention. (By "shape" I mean the whole essence: not just form, but style, tone, pace, etc.) We recognize it, we understand it, and if we don't, then something is wrong with the work, i.e., it tries to be shapeless (though in the nature of things this is impossible), or the intention itself is confused or mixed.

As I said at the beginning, we are in the realm of relativity. Borderline cases exist where the intention, though clear, is multiple. I don't mean the layering of esthetic effect intended by serious works of art such as *Madame Bovary*, for instance, which announces its intention within the first ten pages, so that one could, if one had the patience, define that intention, never with complete accuracy, but nevertheless with sufficient accuracy. Its esthetic seriousness is never in doubt. The same with a hard-sell advertisement for a newfangled wrench on cable TV: it may induce a somewhat mixed effect (shock, indignation, greed, etc.), but its commercial seriousness is never in doubt. That is its clear intention. The intention of an advertisement for whiskey or perfume in the *New Yorker*, on the other hand, may quite distinctly mingle some esthetic seriousness with its commercial seriousness. Even the alligator on the shirt, I suspect, was designed with a little more, even if only a minim, than a merely commercial intention.

Why an alligator, incidentally? An alligator is "either of two broad-snouted crocodilians of the genus *Alligator*, found in the southeastern U.S. and eastern China." If I may say so, that does not have a hell of a lot to do with shirts. But isn't the point precisely that the effectiveness of images is in part a function of their arbitrariness? Not only Rimbaud knew this, but Homer. The truth is that the alligator is a more effective image than Smokey the

Bear, as the Forest Service has discovered, just because the bear does possess some apparent relationship to the meaning it is intended to convey. The impact of this particular image of the alligator on the human mind is uncluttered, and its lodgment in human memory is disconnected from all associations except the shirt. Anyone who has once come to know it will remember it always. This is what the advertising agency wanted, and all artists will recognize and accede to the technique. Beyond this, moreover, is the mysterious attraction of images of animals exerted upon the human imagination from far, far back. Aesop, the brothers Grimm, Disney, etc. Perhaps, as Clayton Eshleman suggests, this is a consequence of the original traumatic separation of human consciousness from animal consciousness, e.g., in the caves of Lascaux. Further, our animal images are always distorted, either more terrifying or more cuddly than the animal itself, and usually they are anthropomorphic in some degree; this is as true in Galway Kinnell's "The Bear," for instance, as it is in "Goldilocks." Another friend of mine, a young woman, yesterday bought a new shirt in Utica, N.Y., and it has a purple horse embroidered on the pocket. I myself once went to the trouble of making a weathervane, instead of scrounging one from the numerous collections of junk in the region where I lived, because I wanted the silhouette of a crow and couldn't find one. And so on, and so on.

What shall we say when the president gets on the tube to defend a policy that is nonsensical on the face of it? His intention is crystal clear to everyone, and it is fraudulent. If the act itself is not fraudulent, then the image is, though really I think any attempt to separate the two would be quibbling. What do I mean by fraudulence? The serious intention to deceive. And ninety-nine percent of the imagery imposed upon the human mind in our society today is seriously intended to deceive. The president, owing to his political power, may be the worst offender, but the fraudulence of politics and commerce is essentially the same and always has been. It merely happens that in our technological era, commerce led the way in the exploitation of means, and politics learned from it. The effect is the same. Massive doles of fraudulence—images containing the serious intention to deceive—have damaged the collective sensibility, perhaps beyond hope of repair.

Notice this, please. I do not say that people have actually been deceived or that therefore what they feel and think is wrong. In some measure this is probably true. But in larger measure, much larger, I think people have correctly understood intentions, and have perceived the fraudulence without being able to deflect it. The result, more and more obvious, is a loss of faith in the power of any imagery whatever, whether visual, aural, or verbal, and not only in works of fraudulent intent but, by contagion, in works of serious esthetic intent as well. The most critical pollution from which we suffer may in the long run turn out to be not in our physical environment but in our emotional and valuational field, in which our civilization subsists just as our planet subsists in its gravitational field. At any rate the erosion of susceptibility to imaginative works is clear and clearly dangerous. We are a society apparently content to live in a condition of moral vacancy, without values, or with only vestigial and largely unexpressed values, because we know that the valuational images presented to us are intentionally fraudulent, and often enough intentionally inane.

Some social critics say that we are complicitous in our own imaginative and valuational demise because we do not exert our own power to command an end of intentional fraudulence by refusing to look and listen. But to my mind this is unproven, to say the least. Has any people ever risen up en masse against a solely cultural oppression? If this were possible, then our entire system of public education, from bottom to top and from one end of the country to the other, would be terminated tomorrow. The great majority of us are aware that the intention of deceit is visible in our schools and universities in many and unmistakable ways. And our children, who are closest to it, are the most aware of all. Yet the system endures. For example, when I visited about a year ago the large elementary school my stepdaughter attends in Syracuse, I was fascinated by the number of times I saw the word "fun": on posters, signs, instruction sheets, the daily mimeographed schedule, everywhere. The school was trying to sell education to the children, trying to compete with TV. But believe me, my stepdaughter is not that easily fooled, and she knows that much of what she is required to do in school is not only not fun, it is stupid. She and her classmates quite evidently react more strongly *against* public education than they would if the school dropped its deceitful advertising and let the education, such as it is, speak for itself. Further, at Syracuse University, where I have been teaching, the connection between the university and the National Science Foundation and the Pentagon is clear and direct; the connection to the atrocious and archaic government in South Africa is only a shade less clear and direct. Similarly, the strongest pitch made to prospective students is that an education at

Syracuse will increase their incomes later on. In the face of all this, tons of flossy propaganda issue continually from the public-relations department in which humane learning for its own sake is made the *primary* reason for the institution's existence. Every-one—faculty, students, administrators, custodians, and alumni—knows this is a deceit. And although my personal experience in the academic trade is brief, I believe this deceit may be found almost everywhere, together with a tacit understanding concern-ing it—which becomes, in effect, an immense conspiracy of self-deceit. What utter folly!

Maybe we should throw in the towel. Plenty of people think so. And it's true that where the evolution of collective sensibility is con-cerned, there seems to be a huge historical determinism at work that cannot be resisted: our whole cultural evolution, as I sug-gested at the beginning, from the early Renaissance to the present. I say "seems to be" because I am not convinced, one way or the other. As a practical matter, not a theoretical one, the question subsumes more factors, cultural, social, and even genetic, than I can hold in my mind at one time. But suppose resistance is impos-sible. Let's go out with clear heads. As long as our intuitions re-main operative—though who knows what the psycho-engineers are planning?—we shall continue to be aware of fraudulent inten-tions in the images given to us in such massive doses that we can-not choose, individually, to reject more than a few of them. Life would be intolerable if we had to make a full act of rejection every time we saw a McDonald's arch, for instance. But at least we can keep ourselves receptive to images of serious imaginative and valu-ational intention wherever we happen to find them. This isn't easy. Plenty of professional artists, the status-seekers, are producing works whose intention is to be less than seriously esthetic. But we know that we are aware of intention, truly aware, and that this is possibly the one element of our inherent freedom as human be-ings which cannot be taken from us. (Even the choice of suicide is more easily constrained.) Let us use all our intuitional power, which is great, to concentrate our awareness of intention, and to act, whenever we can, in accordance with that awareness.

At least then we will understand what images are valid and which kinds of waste are humanly defensible.

PERSONALITY OF GENIUS

One of the finest things that ever happened in the history of any art occurred in this country in 1938 when Alan Lomax invited Ferdinand Morton to come to the Library of Congress and record some of the songs he remembered from his childhood in New Orleans in the nineties. Morton came for an afternoon and stayed for a month. Singing, talking, playing fragmentary chords or complete compositions on the concert grand at which he sat, reminiscing, thinking out loud, Morton told his story, much as he might have told it to a group of youngsters around a parlor piano. Instead, he told it to a recording machine, and we have as a result a remarkably fine document. It has obvious historical value and it gives us some lucky additions to the recorded work of a great piano player; but above all it is a study in the personality of genius.

Like so many geniuses, Morton was not a person one would choose for a friend. His story is a complex of ego and anxiety, full of petty meanness and jealousy. If one wishes to be absolutely honest and at the same time brutal, one says that it is a record of lying, cheating, pimping, and protesting. It is; yet the genius comes through, not only in the music, not only in Morton's account of his early accomplishments—an extravagant account to say the least—but especially in his incidental statements and in the very tone of his voice, so warm and rhythmical, full of unconscious poetry. The thirst for music is always there, and more than that the thirst for creation, the single-minded drive to make something beautiful and meaningful. There were other geniuses in those early years of jazz, perhaps a good many, but certainly Morton deserves a lion's share of the credit for transforming the Creole folk music of New Orleans into a genuine art form, disciplined, lucid, human, true to its own tradition.

This book is composed of two main narratives. Morton's early years—his childhood, his experience as a young musician in the south, his life in California, his first recordings—are set down in his own words, abridged and edited from the Library of Congress records. Much of the flavor is lost in transcription, not the least of it being the entire running accompaniment of the piano, but enough remains to convey the authenticity of the original. The second part of the book is an account of Morton's last years in the words of Mabel Bertrand Morton, his second wife. Between the chapters are "Interludes," in which Lomax tells of his attempts to test and amplify the accounts given by Morton and his wife, mostly reports of interviews with Morton's relatives and with other musicians.

This method is all right as far as it goes, but it doesn't go far enough. Lomax has turned up a few new details of the musician's life, but as a biography the book contains conspicuous gaps. One need only look at the discography appended to the text to find these gaps. The discography lists, for instance, the records Morton made with the New Orleans Rhythm Kings, yet the text does not once mention his association with these white musicians, which was important in more ways than one. Morton's exceedingly active period from 1925 to 1930, when he made his greatest contribution to the development of jazz, is hastily told. But the book's most serious flaw is its lack of any serious analysis of what Morton actually did, his achievement as a musician.

The fault lies fundamentally in Lomax's attitude toward his subject. In his attempt to justify Morton's life to the public he has gone overboard; he has produced a popularization, to my mind a cheapening. Throughout, Morton is called by his absurd commercial nickname, "Jelly Roll." Lomax's writing is highly colored and suffers from imprecision. Everywhere the attempt is made to treat Morton as a folk hero and to capitalize on his foibles. Well, Morton was a folk hero, and a colorful and eccentric person, but he was also an artist. He deserves, and needs, something far better than this kind of "appreciation," one of the many that the commercial press has let loose in the past decade to capture the growing market of jazz enthusiasts. Lomax's account is condescending, consciously or unconsciously, and in two ways. When an author condescends to art, that is bad enough; when he condescends to race, it is intolerable. A more valuable project in the long run would have been a verbatim publication of the Library of Congress records.

TOM MCGRATH IS
HARVESTING THE SNOW

After the war, in 1946 or possibly 1947, I first encountered the poems of Tom McGrath in Shag Donohue's bookstore on 57th Street in Chicago. I had been born an easterner, but from the back hills of New England, not the city, and I had a mixed heritage anyway. My grandfather had founded the first newspaper in the Dakotah Territory in 1885; my father had been born in Sioux Falls. My grandfather told me of hearing Bryan and of working with Debs in the years before World War I. In other words I had a pretty good dose of prairie populism in my childhood, and actually it fitted quite well with the eighteenth-century libertarianism of the hillside farmers who were my neighbors. Naturally McGrath's poems appealed to me.

But I was puzzled too. Why wasn't McGrath a fixture in *Partisan Review*, for instance, or the *New Leader?* Why wasn't he right in there with Delmore Schwartz and the rest of the gang? He wasn't, of course. Even though he hewed close to the CP line in his poems of the late thirties and during the war, McGrath was still a flyweight corn-hoer to the élite. Do you remember Pound's remark— he who had been born in Idaho—about Harriet Monroe with "the prairie dust swirling in her skirts"? Unless one ascribes rank ingratitude to Pound, which would seem an overreaching, the remark has less to do with Harriet than with some of the poets she published: Sandburg, Lindsay, Neihardt, who were absent from the *Little Review, Vortex, transition*, etc., as McGrath was absent from *Partisan*. The New York radical élite, oriented toward Europe, had always ignored "native" radicalism, I mean the continuous tradition of the élite from Johann Most to Alexander Berkman to Philip Rahv. What a pity! I am as strong for upholding literary standards as anybody, but why should *Partisan* have given us so much warmed-over Sartrean engagement when the conditions of the American working class and intelligentsia were so obviously different? What did Sartre know about the HUAC? And why was *Partisan* so damned eager to publish poems by T.S. Eliot and not Tom McGrath, to say nothing of Dr. Williams?

A significant attempt, perhaps partly unconscious, was made to subvert the tastes and opinions of my generation of American youth, and it largely succeeded.

But not with McGrath. He continued writing, he published his poems wherever he could, he refined his radicalism, moving away from Marxist simplicity toward a functional American anarcho-socialism, and he extended the scope of his poetic vision. For a time he lived on the West Coast and was, at least so I infer, turned on to the pseudo-radical antics of California's senile babies; but his roots were always in the plains. The harsh land had made his sensibility: stone and gravel, wind and snow, rust and poverty. And in the end his sensibility remained faithful to the land. He moved back to Dakota. I don't know exactly when that was, but I think perhaps around 1968.

Let me make it clear that I'm not talking about some social-realist hack. I'm talking about a poet with as great a voice as Whitman's, and with a devotion to the American language (and its English antecedents) the equal of anyone's. A superb talent, a splendid imagination. A *poet*. I give myself the credit of recognizing that from the first; and when I made my anthology (*The Voice That Is Great within Us*), I tried to indicate it by giving McGrath as much space as most of his contemporaries, Jarrell, Berryman, and the rest. But I've yet to see another anthologist who has picked up the cue, and only very infrequently do I meet young poets who know what McGrath has done.

He has persevered. He has been fantastically consistent, loyal to himself. Here is a poem, a late one, called "Ordonnance":

During a war the poets turn to war
In praise of the merit of the death of the ball-turret gunner.
It is well arranged: each in his best manner
One bleeds, one blots—as they say, it has happened before.

After a war, who has news for the poet?
If sunrise is Easter, noon is his winey tree.
Evening arrives like a postcard from his true country
And the seasons shine and sing. Each has its note

In the song of the man in his room in his house in his head
   remembering
The ancient airs. It is good. But is it good
That he should rise once to his song on the fumes of blood
As a ghost to his meat? Should rise so, once, in anger

And then no more? Now the footsteps ring on the stone—
The Lost Man of the century is coming home from his work.
"They are fighting, fighting"—Oh, yes. But somewhere else.
   In the dark.
The poet reads by firelight as the nations burn.

Notice how the tenderness for the poet winds into McGrath's desperate anger, almost disillusioned anger. Yet he perseveres. The
poem is in hard-sounded prosody, done with perfect verbal tact.
This is the poet at work, the poet transmuting his political and
social anxieties into *memorable* structures. I emphasize memory.
Isn't that what art wants, to make politics a part of culture? Homer could have and would have made as much of Daniel Shays as
he did of Odysseus. But the poet today has many voices. Here is a
poem called "When We Say Goodbye":

It is not because we are going—
Though the sea may begin at the doorstep, though the
   highway
May already have come to rest in our front rooms . . .

It is because, beyond distance, or enterprise
And beyond the lies and surprises of the wide and various
   worlds,
Beyond the flower and the bird and the little boy with his
   large questions

We notice our shadows:
Going . . .
—slowly, but going,
In slightly different directions—
Their speeds increasing—
Growing shorter, shorter
As we enter the intolerable sunlight that never grows old or
   kind.

Notice here the remarkable rolling control of the long lines. As I
have said, Whitmanian. You cannot find more than a few American poets who can do this, though the ephebe says it is easy. Notice also the sentiment, very congenial to a fellow northman, that
says the sunlight is intolerable. Is this not the hardihood that old
radicals and young poets, who are the same, must assimilate to
their deepest impulses? In spite of everything, the whole goddamn mess, McGrath says:

> I'll have to walk out in the snow
> In any case. Where else is there to turn?
> So if you see me coming, a man made out of ice,
> Splintering light like rainbows at every crazed joint of my
>   body,
> Better get out of the way: this black blood won't burn
> And the fierce acids of winter are smoking in this cold heart.

No, we have nowhere else to turn, McGrath and I, though we have
never met and when we die our graves will be far apart. But they
will be among the speaking graves, the orating graves, sounding
forth from beneath the heavy depths of snow. Watch out, all you
smushy flatlanders. Fold your dewy palms, and listen to the brilliant voice of midnight.

AUTHENTICITY IN
THE AGE OF MASSIVE,
MULTIPLYING ERROR

In a book I was reading the other night—Wendell Berry's *Standing by Words*—I found this sentence: "We must not be misled by the procedures of experimental thought: in life, in the world, we are never given two known results to choose between, but only *one* result that we choose without knowing what it is." Nothing new in this, one says, accepting it; nor did Berry intend an original idea. Indeed it is hardly an idea at all, but simply a token of changed attitudes that affect everyone in this age of, e.g., patent medicines that have been tampered with. What Berry wanted was to indue the notion with the intensity of his own feeling and the clarity and concision of his own language. He has succeeded very well, it seems to me, as he usually does.

What struck me, what is likely to strike many readers of my generation, is the way Berry's formulation impinges on the practical philosophy of forty years ago. Existence before essence, we used to declaim. Authenticity, we said—hurling it in the face of absurdity. Mankind's assertion of value in a valueless *milieu*, whether cosmic, social, or private, through the free operation of human intelligence. And so on; the terms were—at least roughly—Sartre's, but the general drift was accepted by a great many thinkers, writers, and plain folk whom we call existentialists (though they themselves often disputed that title). It was a widespread rediscovery of free will as a theological concept that could be inverted to validate human existence in a world from which all other theological structures of thought had suddenly, i.e., in the prior century, been expunged. And I don't think this necessarily reductive summation is discountable on the ground that many noted theologians—Tillich, Niebuhr, Buber, Marcel, etc.—worked within the main alignments of existentialist feeling or that Kierkegaard, a distinctly religious writer, was assigned a founding role in the development of existentialist attitudes by everyone who shared them.

Someone has said that a historian is an inverted prophet. In almost the same way writers and artists are inverted mystics: they extrapolate from spiritual experience the artifacts that can be put back into the world as objective representations of value. At any rate it was notable that artists and writers took readily to the new understanding of free will and authenticity because it seemed to be practically operative in their own acts of creation. And in fact free will was—and is and always will be—a powerful factor in the appeal exerted by the imagination and its works upon our attention.

Notice Berry's words carefully. He chose them with care, and they deserve to be read in the same way. Although he is arguing against technological and experimental ways of thought, although he urges the usefulness of convention and form in practical as well as intellectual life, although he often uses the language of ordinary conservatism, and although he is doing these things, more and more in his recent writing, in terms of his own quite simple, but never simpleminded, Christianity, his statement is by no means a glib dismissal of science, technology, bureaucracy, or even agribusiness, such as we have come to expect from the "ecology movement"—Berry himself puts the term in quotes. On the contrary, he would say that all these bugbears, even agribusiness, are natural and necessary if properly understood, which means properly—*proprietively*—limited. In his endeavor to hew to the line of propriety, Berry uses language that is fundamental, words that undercut apparent philosophical incompatibility.

For myself, I have never doubted that the predicament of technological society *in extremis* is more the consequence of Hegel's ideas than of Francis Bacon's.

Berry says *choose*—which is what Sartre said. Berry and Sartre are not in conflict, though at first they appear to be. But Berry lays his emphasis not upon choice as an act of intelligence, but upon choice as *commitment*. He says expressly that we must choose what we cannot know, yet still we must choose. He means this in a perfectly worldly sense. The poet who chooses a phrase or an image cannot know until long afterward whether it will succeed in the particular place given it. A man or woman who chooses a mate in marriage cannot know if the other person will turn out to be a suitable partner in the long run; in fact the increasing rate of divorce seems to show that the chance is getting more chancy all the time. And anyone who has bought a car lately knows that the auto industry has reduced the scope of intelligent choice to where you want the ashtray, and nine times out of ten you can't even get the color you prefer if it isn't ready to hand on the dealer's lot. Hence Berry abandons the Sartrean notion that intelligence can assert itself *functionally*, in or out of the world. But since we do have minds, and since our animal instincts are vestigial and obscure, he would say, I think, that in choosing we use our minds *for what they are worth;* that is, for examining forms and conventions and for then committing ourselves to a particular course within them.

We choose what we cannot know. We commit ourselves to an imperceivable outcome. (We demonstrate at the gate of our neighborhood nuclear reactor.) Intelligence has very little to do with it. Moreover, although Berry does not say this (as far as I know), fundamentally we make our choices less as human beings than as vital beings, one species among the many that are animate. It is not a question of the value of humanity, but of the value of life, the whole "ecosystem." For me this means equivalence; one kind of life is neither more nor less valuable than another. I could never be a vegetarian, for instance, except on explicitly sentimental grounds, because I can see no fundamental distinction between eating a cow and eating a broccoli: the condition of vitality is precisely that all life feeds on all death. For Berry, however, equivalence is not the case at all, since he expressly assigns differing values to the "hierarchy" of inspirited things that reaches from germs to rats to people to angels to God. This is intrinsic in his notion of propriety as the mode that ought to govern human conduct toward the rest of existence, supplanting egotism. Well, I am not a Christian, and the extension Berry makes from his basic position toward conventional Christianity is one ground upon which we disagree. But notice that with Berry, at least in his writing so far, Christianity derives from his observation of his place in this world as a poet and a farmer, not, as with so many angry, frustrated Christians today, the other way around. Berry and I have other disagreements too, but we share far more than we dispute. That the agony of choice, whether mindful or unmindful, is what distinguishes the living from the dead, and not inventiveness or a desire for expediency: upon this we agree completely. And that from this it follows that the only alternative to suicide, the only way to assert a positive value against a negative one, is to choose the course which we *think*—or feel or imagine or whatever—may give us the opportunity to make further choices: upon this I believe we also agree. To will is *ipso facto* to choose, and to endure is to make many choices; that is, to ensure the continuity of the will. To express our sense of ourselves as enduring creatures, we make sentences—or sing the blues.

This is the practical outcome of my lifetime of choosing, almost always blindly. It is an outcome that has been retrospectively disclosed to me many times, but never more clearly than in Wendell Berry's sentence, which for me reconciles my youthful need for authenticity with my experienced recognition of blindness and error. I recommend it to anyone, but especially to young people— my children and grandchildren, my students, and others—who tell me again and again that they have no means of knowing what to do with their lives.

MICHIGAN WATER:
A FEW RIFFS BEFORE DAWN

(In memory of Richard Wright)

1.
This hour is best, darkening
in absences; loud lights quieten
in a room in a city in the West.

Hour of calm, hour of silences,
silence lingering between the beats;
hour of distances, hour of sadnesses.

Listen, the softly thinking drum
measures the silence in which the bass
murmurs to make the meaning come.

Tranquilly my fingers contemplate
the bone they are, the bone they meet—
these keys breathing among shadows.

Silence holds the sweetness in the tune.
But now who cares? Will our affection,
the great slow sound, tell anything?

Visionaries sauntering in the sound,
you ten well-drunken in dark and light,
sing well, define, dream down the land.

What in the hour, and what in the heart
of sadness, sings in the song's shadow?
Sweet silence, is it then Chicago?

2.
Define. So the drum commands,
so the bass entreats. Define.
Ten black men setting out to dine.

Food of heaven had they none,
food of hell was so damned sweet
they sought and sought, and they had none.

The rope, the knife, the stone, the gun,
the train, the door, the cave, the tree,
the sign, the shutter, the snow, the dead.

Impossible to see, impossible!—
in the lake a wheel turning,
in the water a flaming wheel turning.

Like drowned rats, sodden in the dawn,
back through the streets they bring him
in dead march, the watery one.

Dawn comes to the city as to a cellar,
always gray, seeping, always gray,
and we call it, naturally, Pain of Day.

At one rotten moment of the light
the room stops, neither day nor night,
the music falters, neither black nor white.

3.
My brother and I, without hope,
set forth upon the city, going
in a white cart drawn by a black goat.

The goat was singing as he must,
my brother and I were not so brave.
The sun hove, shaken in his lust.

We stopped now here, now there
at rusty doors to take upon us
Godspeed and the departing cheers.

They gave us gifts of huge sums
of money. One gave his old coat.
Another gave his old fat wife.

"Good-bye, good-bye." We went on.
We were hungry. Near the airport
in a field we killed and ate the goat.

Nothing whatever happened, except
my brother who had been weeping smiled
and I who had been smiling wept.

Hence, scorched in that field, we knew
we were successful. When we returned
indeed the people gave us angry faces.

4.
Listen, in night's last tender hour,
listen, the somewhat stronger beating—
Chicago, our only city, speaking.

Steel: Shall I not, my children,
grow ever brighter, stiffening
against you my abominable beauty?

Concrete: Ah, I crumble! Back
to earth, sterile, changed,
a hundred lives at every crack!

Glass: Thought you would build a
museum case to house you? True enough,
I'll gleam forever. Wait and see.

Chrome: Even I, in my tarnish,
will stay forever in my opposition
to you: I can never diminish.

Brick: Your fathers knew something of touch
and skill and excellence in shaping,
something of gratitude; but not much.

All: Wind, water, stars, and all things
hard and mindless are our company.
Make your music; the night was long.

5.
My Chicago, city of all
the world, strewn
humble-jumble on a wild lakeshore.

We had at one time a beast,
a gorilla, famous among men,
and we kept it at the Lincoln Park Zoo.

In the heart of the city we had a beast
famous among men for power,
natural beauty, pride, and malevolence.

Its eyes bloomed like unlucky flowers
in a rock-cleft face, nodding in the wind
of emptiness nowhere beyond the cage.

The beast died prematurely of a heart
attack; which is to say, of fear.
And it was mourned almost everywhere.

The sun will shine in my back door
some day. But Lord the beast is taken,
taken Lord, taken and taken away.

Listen, the lake waters are seeping
in a thousand conduits, creeping
under the pavement. Listen.

6.
In the cage no word is spoken,
no power of darkness
covers the eyes with forgetting.

In the cage no amnesty
waits in the government of the days,
no behoof, no behest.

In the cage no listener hears
these superb particular concussions
of blood, neither a brother nor a sister.

In the cage the moon is irrelevant,
the sun unintelligible,
and the constellations unrecognizable.

In the cage laughter is courage
and courage is laughter and laughter
is courage is laughter is—*the cage!*

In the cage knowledge is the cage
and the comfort of knowledge
is an exceedingly narrow comfort.

Days succeed and fail. What more?
Nothing, except the murmured "no"
after the clanging of the door.

7.
Gray dawn seeping through stone—
see, the room blenches. Let the beat
intensify. Between bone and bone

the little blood aches with rain
and the tones deepen. Music!
Given all to Saint Harmony, all,

the pain, the awareness of the pain.
That is all. Music is heard
in one heart, harmony's great chord

in one conscience only; and yet
there is this not explained reaching,
touching, extending, as if the pain

could gather each of us to its own
being. Is it possible? The drum
murmurs against the graylight dawn,

the bass, in unison now, is calm,
the piano descends firmly. Chicago,
city of our music, the long "no,"

listen; the night was a good song;
and we are a true city, rising
in the unjust hour, honorable and strong.

THREE
PARAGRAPHS

A day   very solid   February 12th, 1944
cheerless in New York City
                      (while I kneedeep
elsewhere in historical war
was wrecking Beauty's sleep
and her long dream)
                    a day (blank, gray) at four
in the afternoon, overheated in the W.O.R.
Recording Studios. Gum wrappers *and* dust
and a stale smell. A day. The cast
was Albert Ammons, Lips Page, Vic Dickenson,
Don Byas, Israel
Crosby, and Big Sid Catlett. (*And* it was Abe Linkhorn's
birthday.) And Milt Gabler
presided beyond the glass with a nod, a sign. Ammons
counted off
                   a-waaaaan,,,   *tu!*

            and went feeling
his way on the keys gently,
                while Catlett summoned

the exact beat from—
        say from the sounding depths, the universe . . .
When Dickenson came on it was all established,
no guessing, and he started with a blur
as usual, smears, brays—Christ
the dirtiest noise imaginable
              belches, farts
                  curses

but it was music
music now
with Ammons trilling in counterpoise.
Byas next, meditative, soft/
then Page
with that tone like the torn edge
of reality:
and so the climax, long dying riffs—
groans, wild with pain—
and Crosby throbbing *and* Catlett riding stiff
yet it was music   music.
(Man, doan
fall in that bag,
you caint describe it.)
Piano & drum,
Ammons & Catlett drove the others. *And* it was done
and they listened *and* heard themselves
better than they were, for they had come

high above themselves. Above everything, flux, ooze,
loss, need, shame, improbability/   the awfulness
of gut-wrong,   sex-wrack,   horse & booze,
the whole goddamn mess,
And Gabler said "We'll press it"   *and* it was
      "Bottom Blues"
BOTTOM BLUES   five men knowing it well   blacks
      & jews
yet music, music   high
in the celebration of fear, strange joy
of pain: blown out, beaten out
a moment ecstatic
in the history
of creative mind *and* heart/   not singular, not the
      rarity
we think, but real and a glory
our human shining, shekinah . . .   Ah,
holy spirit, ninefold
I druther've bin a-settin there, supernumerary
cockroach i' th' corner, a-listenin, a-listenin,,,,,,,
than be the Prazedint ov the Wuurld.

THE DEFEATED
GENERATION

Is some kind of affirmation implicit in any creating? I believe so. And I believe the history of western art from the Renaissance to the present could be recounted in terms of a continual testing of that affirmativeness. This would be a big job, the kind that takes years, the kind that we propose with a good deal less confidence than our grandparents did, but it might yield a view of our one-directional history that would be unusually clear and useful.

What this means is nothing strange. It is a commonplace of esthetic experience, whether the artist's or the spectator's (though, significantly, we have no satisfactory general term for the "recipient" in the artistic transaction). A negative thought or feeling becomes affirmative *in the act of* its embodiment as a work of art. That is, a negative thought or feeling becomes affirmative when somebody writes it or paints it or sings it, when somebody expresses it. The only true negative is silence, absence. Granted, in exceptional circumstances silence may be eloquent, if anyone is around to notice it. But far more often silence means defeat, only defeat. Thus a defeated person, whose condition is nothing but negative, may, by articulating that condition in a more or less durable expression—lasting, say, more than a minute—give his or her defeat an affirmative aspect. To act is to assert, one way or another, human solidarity in the processes of nature, to live. To do nothing is to die.

Many, many times the words of the blues have made the point that even the slowest, draggiest, saddest, most despairing blues gives a kind of joy to the performer and to the sensually aware listener.

I have emphasized process, rather than product, because the quality that is affirmativeness derives from process, not from product. Many people have said the opposite, that value reposes only and precisely in the work of art itself, not in the act of the artist, and they have used such notions as completeness and order to designate such value. This was the modernist opinion of forty years ago, and in the endlessly shifting muddle of our feelings about art we do not wish to jettison the important insights it contained. Perhaps in recent years we have gone too far in taking our attention away from the work of art, away from its meaning, and have concentrated too much on linguistic, political, and other such matters. Nevertheless I think the basic value of art resides in the act, not in the object. It, the act, is what affirms our capacity to create or discover other values and to understand them.

Once the artists of the Renaissance gave up the fixed values of earlier times and the conventional signs which conveyed them—Yeats' Byzantium, which certainly never existed, however, in the clarity he gave to it—art moved persistently in the direction of greater verisimilitude, the attempt to locate reality, including the substance of dreams and other psychic experiences. But since reality is at odds with human wishes, always and necessarily, this movement toward "realism" has placed in question the affirming value of creative acts even within the acts themselves, which in turn has produced a tension that at times made the act seem impossible. Creation in human terms became a self-contradiction, the internal conflict of art and reality. The idea of completeness, for example: how can it be brought into consonance with reality, which is always incomplete? Victorian novelists used to tack on a chapter at the end to tell what became of the people in the novel after the end of the story. It was an attempt to bring the imagined text back into the "structure" of reality, which is a lack of structure. For obvious reasons it didn't work. Yet an act does imply its own ending, and an artist who undertakes the act without a regard for its ending, even if the ending is in effect no ending, will be making a commitment to disaffirmation, to an impossible act, to silence.

This is exactly what some people do, as my experience in teaching has shown me.

I began teaching in 1972, though in only a small way. A few students, four or five, with whom I met individually in a secluded room. Nevertheless it was real teaching of a sort, and the students were real students, enrolled in a local college in northern Vermont. They got credit, so called, for studying with me. Mostly they were very young and very unsophisticated girls and boys from the farms and villages of the upcountry hills. Later I stopped teaching for a while. Then in 1979 I accepted a professorship, so called, in the graduate writing program at Syracuse University, where my students have been older and more experienced, though not necessarily better educated, than the young people of the Green Mountains. Of course I have taught altogether only a smattering, probably no more than fifty or a hundred, out of the masses of writing students in our colleges and universities during the past decade. But one thing unites them all: they were born after 1945. They came to consciousness in what we call the atomic age, and they have lived their whole lives in an awareness of ultimacy. Technological madness, corporate irresponsibility, terrorism, the decay of social trust (without which no society, however regulated, can endure), and the fragility of intelligent existence have been their daily bread.

I have thought about these people a good deal, as all teachers do. I know a dozen or more ways to point out the unifying attitudes that have sprung from their experience. One way, which I think is as valid as any, is to say that in their art and writing they have trouble with endings. They do not know how to conclude.

Let's suppose that *Finnegans Wake* is the pinnacle of one movement which began in western art with the Renaissance, the movement toward an art that is parallel to, but separate from, reality. I know, many other works of literature, to say nothing of paintings, sculptures, musical compositions, and so on, may be said to have equal importance, but permit me for the sake of discourse to insist on *Finnegans Wake*. First, it is epical in its aims and dimensions, thus fulfilling a fundamental drive of humanist art to recover and reinforce its nearly mythic origins; *Finnegans Wake* is epical in the same way that the *Iliad* and *Paradise Lost* are epical. Secondly, however, *Finnegans Wake* is self-enclosed and self-sustaining, to such an extent that it takes years to make oneself at home in it, and even to such an extent that the majority of us who acknowledge its greatness have never made that effort and in fact do not understand the book except in the most general way. Thus *Finnegans Wake* fulfills another fundamental evolutionary drive in western art. I don't mean toward unintelligibility, though I wouldn't much blame anyone for thinking this. I mean toward the idea of the masterpiece as a continually refined artistic objective over the centuries. A masterpiece is a work that aims to be undeconstructable and very nearly is. Whereas one cannot read Homer's epic without a broad though shallow knowledge of the preclassical culture of the eastern Mediterranean, and whereas one cannot read Milton's epic without a smaller but deeper knowledge of a particular external scheme of values and frame of narrative reference, i.e., biblical Christianity, and whereas one cannot read the epical works of late nineteenth century desperation— *The Dynasts, The Master Builder, Also Sprach Zarathustra,* and many others—without a quite profound and specialized knowledge of the cultural and spiritual specifications of that age, one can, on the other hand, read Joyce's epic without any external knowledge, properly speaking, at all. This was Joyce's intention, and I believe it was in large part his accomplishment. What is required of the reader is an enormously specialized technique of reading, but not much else. The vector of reliance on external reality has been narrowed almost to the vanishing point, and the novel is like a pyramid resting on its apex rather than on its base. *Finnegans Wake* is a dream, and like all dreams it has its own dissociated structure and logic, turned inward. (This last, the turning inward, is what disqualifies earlier dream visions, which could not achieve such psychological verisimilitude; which is to say that their authors had not read Freud's *Interpretation of Dreams.*) It is a huge combination of words, many of which are, granted, allusive, but always the allusion is to other words, to other imaginative tokens, and these, however rooted they may originally have been in other texts, are drawn into the novel and assimilated there so completely, and are so thoroughly reconstructed in the novel's own internal cross-referencing, that they may be understood without recourse to concrete external data, to reality. All one needs is a multilingual dictionary. Even then the lexicographical definitions will serve as no more than clues to the meanings of the words in the novel, which have been forced on them, often in multiplex combinations, by the centripetal power of the work itself.

Some critics who were prominent when I was young asserted that works like *Finnegans Wake* constituted a "new reality" or an "anti-reality," but they were wrong. And wrongheaded. If we are to keep ourselves sane, surely we must hang onto the difference between reality and imagination.

Joyce's novel is a total work of total imagination. It is a human totality, yet still the work of one mind, not of the commonality. It is not a historical response but a temperamental invention. However bleak much of its substance may be, it is still, by virtue of its existence, the supreme incorporation of human hope in a human artifact. Indeed nothing of its conveyed substance is of much importance. Its existence, its self-sustaining thereness as a complex verbalism, a masterpiece, an affirmation, is what counts. Indeed the work abounds in references, often indirect or falsely modest, to itself and especially to itself as autonomous, perhaps nowhere more clearly than at the end: "Whish! A gull. Gulls. Far calls. Coming, far! End here. Us then. Finn, again! Take. Bussoftlhee, me-memormee! Till thousendsthee. Lps. The keys to. Given! A way a lone a last a loved a long the   ," and there it hangs on the smallest, softest word in the language, which incorporates all the rest. What a feat of rhythmic, echoing, punning vocalism. Language is all!—meaning both its phonemic concreteness and its patchwork of significances. Joyce himself once remarked to a friend: "Je suis au bout de l'anglais."

After totality, after the masterpiece—and I repeat that I am speaking of *Finnegans Wake* as exemplary—comes only breakdown. The secular European existentialists of mid-century tried to move the affirmation implicit in consciousness back from imagination to perceived reality. They tried to reconnect the work of art to the historical field of values, meaning morality, and to make artists responsible again. Camus' rebellion, Sartre's freedom and authenticity, Buber's I and Thou, Berdyaev's transcending personality, and so on: they were all attempts to erect from human suffering and ignorance and metaphysical inconsequentiality a kind of bedrock human assertiveness that partook ultimately in affirmation. For them art was not a thing, an object, a masterpiece, but an action, a continuity of human assertion in the face of the meaningless, never self-sustaining but instead significant only and precisely in its ongoing expressive derivation from human suffering. And I must say that for me, born in 1921 and a veteran of World War II, a very ill and bewildered person indeed, my survival was immensely abetted by these ideas, which three decades ago I applied to myself completely. Yet last year, when I taught a graduate seminar in Camus, at the end of the semester one of my students said: "What a crock! It's perfectly evident that Sisyphus is *not* happy. And as for freedom to choose, existence before essence, and all that, in the real world it's a fantasy, and everybody knows it." Looking back then on my own life from the vantage of old age, perceiving all the ways in which my own courses of action and even of thought had been determined and unfree,

I had to concur. I laughed, thinking of the way Sam Johnson kicked the gatepost, or whatever it was, in sufficient refutation of Berkeley's idealism. The realism of the existentialists, upon which they insisted so resolutely, is what comes round to defeat them.

How does this happen? How is it that those who wished forty years ago to desanctify the imagination, reduce it from the vatic role it had acquired in the romantic idealization of human intelligence from the fourteenth century to the early decades of the twentieth, how is it that these writers are today derided as Humanists by the advocates of deconstructivist criticism, those who now call themselves Theorists? This is an old Marxist ploy, of course, though Theorists are not all necessarily Marxists; yet for most of them, anyone who is anti-Hegelian enough to speak up for individuated consciousness is a *de facto* Humanist with a capital H. Well, name-calling is not discourse and ultimately is unimportant. What is important is just the experience of individuated consciousness that the existentialists were talking about, and we know that in reality we *are* collectivized, we *are* depersonalized, we *are* enslaved and corrupted and inauthentic, and all the "freedom" we have inside our skulls is *not* enough to afford us any reasonable plane on which to exist. We may disacquiesce until we are blue in the face, but we are still at the mercy of every power in and out of the universe. In short, the existentialists were as right in their intentions as all philosophers are, including the Marxists, but in their technical, so-to-speak professional adumbrations of theory they foundered, again like all others, on the radical incompatibility of intelligence and actuality. The question of art and reality is at the root of every problem, and it is unanswerable.

What good is a mind which can ask questions that it cannot answer? No one can benefit from it, and no one can turn it off either.

This is what young people today see clearly. What affirmation is possible now, in writing or anything else? The imagination may be powerful, it obviously is, but in the face of threatened extinction and its related terrors—depersonalization, demoralization, radical disorientation, etc.—in the face of human history, that Juggernaut, what is imagination's value? Not only Hegelians understand that the dialectic of mental evolution is irreversible. If we sing the blues, as we do, and our voices go out into the universe in waves of noise forever, what is the point of it? And who cares if the waves are affirmative or not?

No, there are no conclusions. Not even the conclusion of inconclusiveness, made so clearly in Kafka's *The Castle*, Paul Goodman's *The Empire City*, or scores of other works. There is only nothing. My students do not know what to do with their poems, their drafts and fragments, nor can I advise them. Someone has said that Ray Carver has succeeded so well with his short stories because he has eliminated the beginnings and endings; he writes only the middles. To the extent that this is reductive and unfair, it is false. Carver is a writer of unmistakable imaginative power. Yet the truth of the judgment cannot be denied either, for in his stories we have primarily, not change or resolution or containment, but merely duration and locus, and even these are represented fleetingly in pieces of dialogue, often seemingly disconnected. Similarly Donald Barthelme has fitted out his "stories" with random events and alternative arbitrary endings, and he expressly denies the efficacious imagination. He devalues it. The works of both writers are popular with my students, and no wonder; they express the futilism of the age. But are they models? Yes, one can always imitate another, older writer, which is how young writers learn. But what will it serve them in ten or twenty years when they have reached their own artistic maturity? What will be left for the imagination to do? This is no question of a transvaluation of values. What a comfortable Victorian idea! It is a question of radical, probably total, devaluation. The work, even in its unfolding, reveals its inadequacy, its inability to carry the affirmation of its mere existence forward to values of any kind, though this is every work's intention. That is, every work struggles willy-nilly toward the condition of the masterpiece, proclaiming its significance in its existence. This much the contemporary artist has retained from the idea of the masterpiece; retained it and inverted it. In ugliness is affirmation. But can anything at all be taken from a work which exists only in its own failure, its own intentional and self-revealing meaninglessness?

The young people are defeated. They are the defeated generation. Most of my former students no longer write. Some, especially the forlorn girls and boys of Vermont, have turned to religion, usually extreme religion: militant fundamentalism on one hand, or passive orientalism on the other. Those who still write do so sporadically, and very few have faith in the validity of what they are up to. Certainly they are not cheered by the critics who profess deconstructivism, metamodernism, etc., that is to say, by the idea that art which is intentionally meaningless still serves a social purpose because it reflects, literally, the meaninglessness of our broken-down social and cultural mechanisms. Such an idea may be useful to certain programmatic critics, but for writers, who cannot adhere to programs and who must get in there and do the solitary work on their hands and knees (as Yeats said), it has no utility whatever.

And is it not possible to say, even after all our tense and pleading lucubrations, that all good reasons ever advanced for writing, all rationales subsumed variously down the ages under Aristotle's delight and instruction, are still and forever valid? The change that occurred in 1945 was not in the human heart, but in circumstances. The great problems—justice, love, death, ambivalence, and peace—are not different but only more urgent. All the more reason to write then, to get on with the work more seriously than ever.

Take it a step further: are reasons for writing needed? Writing and sex are the same, considered as spontaneous acts of the human animal, and anyone who demands reasons for doing either is—well, perhaps demented, but more likely overdomesticated. Like a Holstein heifer awaiting the capsule.

Which is not to say that both writing and sex aren't amenable to enrichment through conceptual inquiries and determinations of many kinds.

Sometimes I think that only we who were aware of life before 1945 recognize the urgency of the need to do what has never been done before, namely, to effect a primal change in the direction of history, to turn aside the Juggernaut. I mean a change toward reason and restraint, and toward the restoration of value. In his remarkable and important essay called "Standing by Words," Wendell Berry writes: "Value and technology can meet only on the ground of restraint." It is true. To do less than one can, to think of others first, etc. Such is the ground; no need to enlarge it here. Yet I have the impression that today our organizations working for demilitarization and denuclearization, i.e., for restraint, for what Berry would call a *proper* functional relationship between human intelligence and the rest of the universe, are supported chiefly by people my age, not by the young. The young are, almost by definition, certainly by historical "necessity," the defeated, the silenced. What we, the elders, must do in the little time left to us is to transmit our awareness of urgency and our understanding of possibilities to the defeated, and this distinctly includes our understanding that issues of poetry and language, however close they may be in concept to issues of peace and restraint, are functionally subordinate. In *King Lear* Edgar says to Gloucester: "Ripeness is all."

That can be translated from the political madness of Lear's time to the political madness of our own very precisely: survival is all.

Myself, I am not defeated. But this is only because I was born in 1921, not 1947. Already by the time I became a soldier the joy of writing had become a need; I was addicted to the procedures of my own sensibility. All the years I then spent in inventing purposes and ends may have been fruitless; in a sense they were, because I no longer believe much in those purposes and ends; yet I don't regret the years. I survived. I am still here, even if I find that, in essence, here is square one. The joy of writing is what keeps me going. And yes, my poems have beginnings and endings. A basketball game has a beginning and ending, so why not a poem? Perhaps a basketball game even has social and cultural usefulness. Many people think so. Not that I'm saying I am not serious in my writing; never that. I dislike Auden's game-theory of literature as much as ever. But a basketball game is a natural process in a natural form, and what it says about human beings is utterly serious. Hence I am serious. I write hard. I do not choose my topics frivolously. After all, a big part of the joy of writing is telling the truth.

THE COWSHED BLUES

Exsurge, gloria mea;
exsurge, psalterium et cithara

Intro
> Intent in the
> night in the
> cone of light
> > writing

Vamp
> Or what's called
> > writing
> though words must come
> throb by throb
> > > through the membrane
> of the great black drum

16 bar theme
> It was a cowshed when he took it
> a one-cow barn beside a brook
> in a cove of alder and birch
>
> floor of plank and rank urine, the wooden
> stanchel worn in a cow's long wintertimes
> heavy   with animal woe
>
> in the back wall
> was a hole
> with a board flap
> hinged on a harness strap

where they shoveled through
the manure
onto the manure pile
once in a while

so he made a window where the hole was
a table and a stove, and sought the grace
words give for love in a writing place

Piano break
  Light on the page and all else
  the raging dark

12 bar theme
  And tonight the shed rides free and the cove
  its alders and birches
  falls downward among the stars

  because intensity does this, a mind
  out of time, out of place—
  body a field of forgotten wars

  and making does this, the breakthrough
  to a great beat throbbing
  in a place without place

  o moment, moment   pure
  he is an undetermined existence
  part of eternity, gone in inner space.

Stop-time chorus, trombone
  Soaring
    on the modes
    of sound
  the modulations

  moving
    over and through
    the pulses
  of his love

known by no name now
   although
   a muse of everlasting
voluptuousness is aware of him

and the particular
   tones follow
   one another
freely   inexorably

Scat chorus
   Cow now . starflow . the slow
   beat . over and over . flies .
   ow . the cords . the blood
   urine and dung . how
   flying . chains in the neck of
   hathor . perpetual beating .
   her womb . beating . hot eyes .
   now . beating . a great flying .
   and pain . and beating . now

Two choruses ad lib, trumpet
   What our people have never known
   but always felt
   in the mystery of the word

   is a force
   contained but not expressed
   spoken and unexplained—

   for meaning falls away
   as the stars in their spirals
   fall from the void of creation

   how simple and how necessary
   this discipline! which is the
   moment added to moment of being

   movement added to movement
   notes in the throat of the horn
   being and being and being

dying, born   and he
is alone, free
creator of what he cannot help but be

Vamp, guitar and bass
   "Holiness," he says
      hearing an unexpected
   modulation:
               at the point of flow
   always this beat, this beat
      repeated
   instant of everything he knows
      now   forever   existing   here
   it must
      be holiness

Out-chorus
   And blues is also
      a crying in the night
   exhaustion, constriction
      in the cone of light

   and he looks up sighing
      to the dark glass
   where looking back at him
      is his father's face

Stop-time bridge, clarinet
   All's fallen back
      back
   collapsing into time
      time

   the beat   of the great drum   is going
      going
   in the wind in the trees
      in the wind in the trees

Ride out, half-time
   It is   his face now
   his own   his

and old in a moment
miseries, histories

his and his father's
reflected   little things
    among others of this earth
    the alders and the birch

Tag, drums
   But the beat remains
   the moment of purity somewhere
   poised on its long
     flow   far out, far in

Tutti
   or on this page fallen
     notations   of remembered song.

THE MAIN THING
ABOUT IMPROVISATION

Jazzmen have always liked to get together and jam. Perhaps not as much now as formerly, since young musicians fostering their "professionalism" tend to look down their noses at it. Too frivolous, they say. But it's a strange word, isn't it—"jam"? Many people, the pop writers, DJs, buffs, etc., have believed that it means something satisfying and good, like blackberry preserves on your bagel. I have a record album called "Jazz-berry Jam." For my part, though I have no idea when, where, or how this word in the vocabulary of jazz originated, I think it means something more like a traffic jam: something competitive, even hostile. A "jam session" is where musicians "cut" one another. Indeed the jargon of jazz is full of threatening and abusive terms, just as it is full of sexual innuendo. Alas for the species that has converted sex from an act of worship to an act of war.

I wonder often about the night at Minton's in the early 1940s when Dizzy Gillespie, a two-eyed, bright-eyed jack, finally cut Roy Eldridge, who was the king. I wasn't there, I don't know what it was like, I don't remember reading anything about it, and for all I know the event is mythical, apocryphal, a variant of a tale from *The Golden Bough*; yet it is the kind of thing that did happen. And for me it endures as a profundity of feeling, a knot of inextricable pathos and awe in the face of change.

No, a jam session is not covered all over with roses, the blooms of joy and freedom. A jam session is where you force the other musicians into a complementary role, so that you can work out your own ideas and, if the ideas are good enough, win the applause and admiration of all who are sitting in. Not always, of course. In New Orleans seventy years ago, as no doubt in Krakow today, friends gathered to play for the fun of it, and we even possess recorded examples, as in the sessions of Chicagoans at Squirrel

Ashcraft's in the 1930s, recorded on aluminum blanks, or the very noisy wire recordings of after-hours sessions with Charlie Parker before he recorded commercially—Parker, a modest man whose playing nevertheless dominated the group.

But the jam session has more often been public, or semi-public, and competitive. Hence it becomes necessary to say something about the real nature of improvisation. In another essay in this book, the one about Russell and Yeats, I have argued that jazz improvisation is paradigmatic of the evolution of all the arts in the twentieth century; if the linkage is not causal, as it certainly wasn't in the early days, it is nevertheless strikingly parallel. Many people, probably those who think a jam session is fruity, use the word "spontaneity" vis-à-vis improvisation to mean utterly unrestrained, utterly new, utterly utter. Granted, the rare moments when an undeliberated idea—word, phrase, color, tone, etc.— springs into one's mind are marvelous; but they are also unreliable, and art is the product of attitudes grounded solidly in the known. Spontaneous does not mean impromptu. Far from it. Nor does it mean new. It means something more like occasional, i.e., springing from an occasion; in effect, thoroughly worked out, or on the verge of being thoroughly worked out; revised, improved, brought to its own fullness of expression; self-consciously and self-confidently experimental; brilliant in its clarity of achieved articulation. Jazz musicians work out their improvisations in jam sessions, but not only there; they do it too on the stand, in rehearsal halls, in studios, at home by themselves, and sometimes—many have testified to this—while walking, driving a car, performing actions distantly related, if at all, to jazz; sometimes even in dreams, which are, no matter what anyone thinks, work. In these ways improvisations grow. And as long as they contain any fresh input, even if only freshness of feeling without new substance (though this would be impossible in actuality), they are spontaneous. What we notice especially about the great stalwarts of jazz, from Sidney Bechet to Steve Lacy, is not that their playing is always new but that it is always, or almost always, enthusiastic.

Isn't this evident also in the late poems of Alexander Pope, for instance, such as "The Epistle to Dr. Arbuthnot"? I believe so. Pope came into his own as *un homme de style*—a persona, a partly contrived and nevertheless natural public image—by improvising, within the simple form of the closed couplet, a whole congeries of rhythmic, phrasal, and textural—i.e., *attitudinal*— mannerisms that could be deployed with a maximum of self-conscious individuality and a minimum of repetitiousness. And as one moves ahead through the mature poetry of Wordsworth, Browning, Yeats, Pound, Williams, Rukeyser, Duncan, Levertov, this becomes more and more evident. In film, in painting and sculpture, in all the arts, it is the same: improvisation within known forms and habituated attitudes, moving usually in the ultimate direction of simplicity.

Improvisation is the privilege of the master, the bane of the apprentice. It is the exercise of sensibility in acquired knowledge. When it becomes too often repeated, either in the work of the master or later in that of his followers, it loses its spontaneity, because nothing of freshness is happening, and then it is over. Done. Time to go on to something else. But even the capacity to recognize the end is knowledge. Taste is knowledge; which is an important equation for many reasons, but not least because it brings into meaningful correspondence the two variables of judgment, quality and quantity—the more knowledge you have the better your taste will be.

Hence what applies to Bach applies equally to Beiderbecke— and to Rembrandt, Rodin, the architect of Notre Dame, Fellini, and any number of other masters; and thus we have stated— restated—an esthetic principle.

Improvisation then is composition, but composition impelled by knowledgeable spirit, what some people, I think mistakenly, call intuition, never by precept or desire for external acclaim—at least not primarily. The jam session (the poetry workshop) can be useful, but only when it constitutes itself as a sanctuary for the individual imagination functioning in procedural self-knowledge. To the extent that it falls short of this, to the extent that it becomes merely competitive, the artists in it will fall short of their potential accomplishment. Like a town, a nation, a world, the jam session coheres only in love.

THE BLUES SCALE

A friend of mine in Vermont is teaching himself to play the tenor. He is by no means new to music; he played trumpet for years, until an accident with a chainsaw—too common in the woods over there—notched his upper lip in such a way that when it healed the scar tissue could not make an embouchure for brass. Seems to work ok for reeds, though. Recently he went down to Boston and shelled out upwards of $1,600 for a Paris Selmer Mk VI, so you can see he is serious. And like a lot of us he has been meditating more about jazz than we did in the days when we played any old way, mean, dirty, righteous, hard, cool, it made no difference, as long as it sounded good to us.

My friend sometimes plays with a musician trained in the conservatory, a pianist. A month ago my friend wrote, saying that the pianist believes the blues scale goes like this:

Root
Second
Third flatted
Third natural
Fourth
Fifth (sometimes flatted)
Sixth
Seventh flatted
Seventh natural
Back to the root

He asked what I thought. Well, I've been brooding about this since childhood, though for years merely in the manner of brooding about a mystery. Then at a later time I'd have said that the pianist's scheme is the product of an academic mind and a fixed-tone instrument, and that the blues scale is more like this:

Root
Second
Indeterminate
Fourth
Problematical
Sixth
Indeterminate
Root again

In other words I'd have said that the blues third, seventh, and sometimes fifth, played in the diatonic or modern European scale, are remnants of a quite dissimilar African mode. They must be slurred; on the piano they must be played flat and natural at the same time, or in quick succession. Some say the blues *cannot be played* on the piano, or the vibes, or any other fixed-tone instrument. But only in this way, by bending them, can we make these notes "fit" in the diatonic scale, whether major or minor.

But if the third, fifth, and seventh, why not the second, fourth, and sixth? And what, in that case, is the root? What is the scale?

These thoughts have led me now to believe that the whole apparatus of European musical conceptualization is inadequate to the blues, radically so. The idea of the scale does not apply. The ideas of note, tone, intonation, playing in tune, and so on, all are antithetical to the African element in Afroamerican music, to such an extent that they must be abandoned, done away with, repudiated. Which, granted, is a very difficult thing to do for most people, including black American musicians, whose musical sensibilities have been trained from childhood in the modes of European hearing from the fifteenth century to the present. Even that favorite term of the musicologists, *microtonality*, does not work, because the slurring or bending of jazz is never an arrested sound for more than an infinitesimal instant, like the last moment of the flight of Zeno's arrow before it plunges into absurdity: you can't hear the one any more than you can see the other.

Once when I was living in a confined situation for a long time I listened to Chinese opera broadcast on station WEVD from New York. At first I could make no sense of it. The operas went on for hours, days, in a way that seemed to my Euroamerican ear totally random. Yet I found myself more and more responsive. That music was expressing a purely musical substance—for I had no idea what the operas were about—in which my sensual apprehension could function. And did, at least tolerably. Perhaps this has helped me now to overturn my thoughts about jazz and the blues.

Every musical person should be required to listen to Chinese opera for a week each year.

A story is told about Eddie Condon that when someone pointed out to him how musicians of the younger generation, meaning the generation of Parker, Gillespie, Powell, etc., played flatted fifths, Condon retorted: "We don't flat our fifths, we drink them." I suspect the story is untrue; but if it is true, then Condon's witticism is simply the kind of nonsense any of us might utter in a foolish moment. One need only listen to the recorded performances organized by Condon himself to hear plenty of flatted fifths and flatted everything else. On some of the records made by young Chicagoans in the late 1920s and early 1930s, featuring such musicians as Teschemacher, McPartland, Freeman, etc., one can find passages in which practically everyone is playing "out of tune." This is what those musicians were famous for, their avid, rugged, headstrong disregard of musical convention in general.

What we are left with then is *pitch*, pitch alone, vibrations per second—the primordial root of all and any musics. And in many of them this means, practically speaking, *variable pitch*. (The analogy with W.C. Williams' *variable foot* is useful if not pressed too far.) The European idea that fixed tones are an advance, a rationalized refinement, a sophisticated methodization, as compared to the "primitive" musics of Asia, Africa, and so on, is cultural chauvinism at its worst (akin to Margaret Mead commanding the "natives" to build her a house), though precisely because we are so "attuned" to it we have difficulty perceiving the unreason of it, the outrageousness. Yet as so often in other sectors, the only view of human mentalism which will serve us here is the one we take *sub specie aeternitatis*.

The "blues scale" therefore cannot be talked about in what are for us conventional terms. It cannot be objectively "notated"—see how I must keep using quotation marks to signify the words no longer meaningful?—except perhaps by some impossibly complicated, computerized oscillograph. It is subjective. It is an understanding that is felt. Is this a monstrous obstacle? Not at all. The understanding can be transmitted by the simplest means, i.e., from ear to ear. Our "notation" is the phonograph record or the electronic tape, the performance. How wonderful! From subjectivity to subjectivity the music of the blues flows unimpeded and, what's more, even assisted by the versatility of mere engineering. If you need a visual equivalent, picture the "blues scale" to yourself as a *glissando,* a slide, beginning anywhere, ending anywhere, and attached to duration, the rhythmic component, by the subtlest imaginable architectonic diversities.

What does this mean for jazz today? I broach my feeling tentatively, because I know my lack of training. But I do think that jazz musicians who have strayed from the blues root, who have been impressed unduly by European conventions in the conservatory, so that they cannot see around them or behind them—which may mean simply those who have been too much influenced by the piano, the instrument of teaching—are on the wrong track. I can hear a music both expressive and progressive in which the idea of playing in tune is irrelevant. Examples are usually dangerous, but I will risk saying that I prefer the line of development I hear in Ornette Coleman, Roland Kirk, Arthur Blythe, and Archie Shepp, as extended by such younger musicians as, say, Dave Holland, to the line I hear in much of Miles Davis and the later John Coltrane. In this respect it is worth repeating the observation made already by Gerald Early, that in retrospect Thelonious Monk seems less a performing musician than a composer, a songwriter. I do not mean to be cryptic. Monk was a genius. Perhaps he is the best example we have in jazz of a piano player trying to escape the confines of his instrument, although that has been the attempt of nearly all jazz pianists since Ferdinand (Jelly Roll) Morton—the piano is the instrument *par excellence* for ragtime, as it is for the compositions of Mozart and Chopin, but it is inimical to the blues. One might argue that the best blues pianist was Basie, who reduced his style to a minimalist melodic phrasing with the primary emphasis on rhythm; yet even Basie (together with some of the musicians associated with him) was more at home in the four-stanza, 32-bar, essentially sonata form of the Tin Pan Alley tune than in the blues. Again and again, at any rate, Monk was driven away from improvisation and toward composition, granting that the two overlap considerably; he made songs that other musicians could perform better with other instruments than he could with the piano. The contrast to Duke Ellington, who had a whole band at his fingertips, so to speak, and a remarkably many-voiced band at that, is illuminating. Ellington's influence is still pervasive, while that of Basie has died away, and Monk's appears to be diminishing.

All this about the piano is intentionally argumentative, that is, exaggerated. But what I have said about the blues is not; I have said it—and before that thought it—in the spirit of our super-rebel, Friedrich Nietzsche, who wrote: "Without music life would be a mistake."

BEN WEBSTER

It was Catlett driving, de Paris blowing strong,
And James P., the incomparable—he could play
Anything. But that day all along
Had been Ben Webster's, as he made that old song
Leap out of itself in greatness, never to belong
To anyone else. Oh, far and wide
The spit sprayed out on either side
Of his number seven reed to create that breathy
Tone, those growls, those flutters,
Which are all most people hear in their deafness;
But it was music, music. What matters
Was oneness, the abstract made personal in a tone,
You in your transcending freedom, never another's
Ever again,
        Ben Webster,   after you've gone.

THE TIME OF
FALLING APART

All of us who are poets of radical thought and feeling—meaning in
practice anywhere left of center; meaning in ideality devoted to
human freedom—must come to terms somehow, if we acknowledge the influence of Ezra Pound's work on our own at all (and I
don't see how very many of us can avoid that)—must come to
terms with his rotten politics, which is a hard job and one that we
aren't ever likely to finish. The human mind is so constructed that
moral issues, if we are honest with ourselves, cannot be resolved.
The conflicts between ideality and practice, between love and justice, are everlasting, at least in finite intelligence. Ideology is a
cop-out.

Such is the wisdom of old men, trite, tedious, unwelcome wisdom, as Pound himself may have come to see in his old age. And
how shall one express it, especially in the twentieth century?
Pound fell into silence, the writing of fragments. Pound was thirty-
six years old when I was born, Sartre was sixteen, and Martin
Luther King, the only public figure in America during my lifetime
with whom I felt I could agree, was minus eight. Yet King was
black and I am white, he was a Christian and I am not, and the
probability is that if we had ever met over a cup of coffee we would
have disagreed. And in any case he was assassinated. What a
crazy time I've lived in!

Pound was crazy too, certifiably so, and friends of mine who
knew him as far back as the mid-1930s have told me that the
signs were evident then. But no one knows how to calculate the
degree of his illness. We cannot use it to explain his politics.
Could the man who wrote

> Forked shadow falls dark on the terrace
> More black than the floating martin
>   that has no care for your presence,
> His wing-print is black on the roof tiles
> And the print is gone with his cry.

—could such a man be said to have suffered from delusive vision, estrangement from reality? (And how many, incidentally, can now tell a martin from a blackbird, or recognize the accuracy and faithfulness of Pound's love of nature?) Think of the ending of his climactic canto (no. 90):

> Trees die & the dream remains
>   Not love but that love flows from it
>   ex animo
>   & cannot ergo delight in itself
>   but only in the love flowing from it.
> UBI AMOR IBI OCULUS EST.

Could such a mind, in its synthesis of felt interpretations, be said to have suffered a failure of reason? A failure of feeling?

Besides insanity, other explanations—excuses—are offered. Pound's élitism, including particularly his antisemitism, was a consequence of the sociology of his life; that is to say, being an American in a culture dominated by European, mostly aristocratic thought and feeling has never been easy, and has produced among poets all kinds of twisting and warping. Granted. Social credit, in its original formulation by Major Douglas, was a quite reasonable attempt to deal with economic injustice (and would do wonders for America today), and only Pound's misapplication and oversimplification makes it reactionary in his writings. Granted. Pound, like many others, was duped by the socialistic pretenses of fascism during its early manifestations. Granted. And there are plenty of other similar explanations.

But none will serve. None. We are left with a bundle of self-conflicted ideas and desires. It will not cohere, as Pound himself observed in his desperate final years. The rage for order is still a rage. But has anyone else done significantly better? It depends on what you mean by "significantly," I suppose, but my feeling is negative. In the long run no one else has done better. Do the clarity of image and power of expression in Pound's poems, which have never been matched by any other American poet, make up for defects of understanding? Again my feeling is negative. The mess of life is more important than the attempted lucidity of art and ideas. Charles Olson's anguished diary of his visits to Pound at St. Elizabeth's represents us all. Pound was a vile and dangerous political advocate, yet the influence of his poetry on *every* segment of American literature today is plain to see. This century, yours and mine, has been a time of falling apart. It will not cohere. We are reduced sometimes to silence, often to fragments. Where true love is . . . true vision . . . , etc.

THE BLUES
AS POETRY

I am not speaking of the part of traditional blues that qualifies as literature on poetic grounds, but of the use of the tradition, both thematically and formally, by poets.

Poets who love the blues are moved quite naturally to try composition in the traditional form. For one thing, the form is another proof—here in our midst—that complex rhyming and metrical schemes, such as, in the past, the French *villanelle* and *triolet*, the *cansò* of the trobadors, the *cansone* and *sonnetto* of northern Italy, do derive ultimately from the folk, no matter how they may be trivialized and overrefined by poets of the aristocracy later on. (Examples even more extreme may be found in Sanskrit, in pre-Mohammedan Arabic poetry, in medieval Celtic, and in many other "primitive" literatures.) That the blues are a folk invention, even in some cases today, is self-evident to anyone who listens to them. That the tradition is a difficult one for poets is only somewhat less than self-evident, since published examples are still both few and inferior a good sixty years, or at least three poetic generations, after the blues were popularized in the 1920s. David Budbill of Vermont has written good blues. June Jordan has poems that remind me of the blues, which obviously was her intention, although as far as I know she has not written an explicit blues. Gwendolyn Brooks has written a few fine blues; Langston Hughes also. Allen Ginsberg has written many blues, unfortunately not fine at all; they sound to me like the very minor, white, watered-down imitation-blues of the Tennessee backcountry, as sung once by Joe Hill and Woody Guthrie. Raymond R. Patterson, in his *Elemental Blues* (Merrick, N.Y., 1983), has written some excellent blues—when I read them I hear lost voices, Ida Cox, Mildred Bailey, Lil Green—and has made a few experiments with variations on the basic form, but to my mind his experiments do not go far enough, and the diction in too many of his poems is sentimental and old-timey. I myself have written a few blues, but none I care to publish. Since I have been playing and singing the blues for more than fifty years, perhaps this is as good an indication of the difficulties as any.

What is wanted is a poem in the conventional three-line stanza, at least to begin with, that can be sung but that can also stand by itself in print, without music, as poetry. The lines should rhyme; the second line should duplicate the first, that is, the refrain, so to speak, should come before the main element of each stanza. Each line should assimilate itself both to twelve beats of music, the underlying measure, and to some shorter, more comfortable rhythmic and prosodic arrangement of spoken language.

Problems, formidable ones, emerge at once. To avoid triteness and tedium in the repeated lines, to impart phrasal variation and appeal to language not strictly metered (though a remarkable number of blues lines do fall into pentameter), to decline the temptation to try for effects that can be accomplished only in music, and so on. Some degree of literariness—and I use the term without deprecation—is almost certainly necessary. In one of her early blues, for instance, Billie Holiday sang the line:

> I ain't good-looking, and my hair ain't curled

The "I" is held for something more than six beats, a beautifully effective musical maneuver. But in literature no punctuation, no typography, not even Robert Duncan's innovative spacings and markings (though they function pretty well in his poetry), can force the reader's eye to linger that long on a single syllable. If you printed the "I" alone on one page, and continued the rest of the line on the next page, or even after twenty blank pages, the reader would still go as immediately as possible to the continuation, and the phrasing enforced by the beat of the music would be lost. It is not a question of what the reader should do, but of what he or she inevitably will do. Responsible writers must take this into account.

Within the boundaries of literature-as-such, however, considerable rhythmic and phrasal variation can be created. Let me set down a few rudimentary observations.

1. Conventional punctuation is of little use. The most critical part of the blues line is the caesura. Very few lines consist of a

single syntactical unit. Hence variation from the first line to the second in each stanza can best be accomplished by moving the caesura, indicating a pause that is either metrical or ametrical; singers do this all the time. But a comma will not suffice in a printed blues, nor will any mark, especially as one reads stanza after stanza. A line break is more effective. Thus the stanza from which I quoted above:

> I ain't good-looking
>   and my hair ain't curled
> I ain't good-looking and my
>   hair ain't curled
> but my mother gave me something it's going to
>   carry me through this world

This is literary, not musical, that is, not exactly as Holiday sang it. But for me it works better than a mere transcription would. No punctuation therefore. How about the hyphens and apostrophes? I think I'd omit them too:

> I aint good looking
>   and my hair aint curled

This appears cleaner and better to me. My friend Joel Oppenheimer would insist that the "I" be lowercase, but on this, though in little else, I disagree with him.

2. The more difficult question arises of whether or not to attempt orthographical reproduction of speech, our literary koine having deviated so far from our pronunciations—or "t'other way abaout," as Pa McCabe used to say. Holiday sang "lookin," not "looking," and in the third line she sang neither "going to" nor "gonna," but "goin to." It is a matter of taste, subjective and relative, and of what one wants to do; and also, inevitably, of one's capacities. Ezra Pound could not write dialect, though he liked to try. Mark Twain could and did. My own thought is that if verse forms arise in the folk, and if, as I said at the beginning, they evolve necessarily toward literature, then the shift from street language to literary usage is not to be deplored, provided the poem does not become pedantic. The artful poet today will in fact use the whole range of diction from vulgar to technical—as Derek Walcott mixes Jamaicanese with the language of Fleet Street.

Such mixtures would be not at all unsuitable to the blues. (Cf. also ballads by Auden, Thomas, Robert Hayden, and many others.)

3. Variations of form have been introduced by the musicians already. Here is another stanza from Holiday's blues:

> my man wouldnt give me no breakfast
>> wouldnt give me no dinner
>> squawked about my supper then he
>> put me outdoors
> had the nerve to lay
>> a matchbox on my clothes
> I didnt have so many
>> but I had a long long ways to go

Then there is the final stanza, in which the four-part first line is rhymed:

> some men like me cause Im happy
>> some cause Im snappy
>> some call me honey
>> others think Ive got money
> some say Billie
>> baby youre built for speed
> now if you put that all together
>> makes me everything a good man needs

(I see no way to write "because" for "cause" without metrical awkwardness in this instance.) With these hints and others, such as the fairly common two-line and four-line stanza in the sung tradition, poets should be able to think of further variations that will augment the formal latencies of the blues.

4. One variation from standard form that at first seems simple—it has occurred to a fair number of musicians and songwriters in the past, e.g., Lee Wiley, Johnny Mercer, etc.—is the use of a stanza with three separate lines and three rhymes:

> well in new york baby
>> you cant hardly ever see the sun
> and in la and miami
>> the fuzz is always reaching for his gun
> lets go to your town baby
>> and just sit and watch that old green river run

One sees immediately that this upsets and weakens the dynamic of structural attitude or expectation in the stanza; repetition seems necessary, though this may be something that poets, rather than songwriters, can work out. Other traditional variations, such as the separation of the first two lines in each stanza while the third line repeats from one stanza to another, which is again close to the lyric tradition of trobador and jongleur, work quite well and indicate directions in which literary development might go.

5. Why bother? Because the blues, altogether aside from their music, are often more expressive than conventional poetry, by which I mean virtually all poetry written in the U.S.A. today.

> blues jumped a rabbit
> run him for a solid mile
> well the blues jumped a rabbit and they
> run him for a solid mile
> rabbit turn over and he
> cry like a little baby child

This goes back at least to 1925, probably to a time earlier than that. Or consider the final stanza of a much later blues, sung by Holiday twenty years after the one I've quoted above.

> love is just like a faucet
> it turns off and on
> love is like a faucet it turns
> off and on
> sometimes when you think its on baby
> it has turned off and gone

Two similes, many years apart, one from rural life and the other from urban, but both naturally related, spontaneously and integrally related, to the common culture around them; yet they are original and inventive too. They are *expressive*. This, it seems to me, is what so much of our poetry has lost. Ginsberg is at least correct in his intention: to get back for our poetry what the blues already and naturally possess. Then notice the purely poetic values in the last stanza quoted, the *modulation*—not rhyme, not assonance—of verbal sound: love/just/faucet/turns/off/on/gone. Such delicacy! Louis Zukofsky did no better, though he did as well.

6. Raymond Patterson has written, in the introduction to his *Elemental Blues*, ". . . the subtleties of this American verse form

have yet, in America, to receive the attention given to the haiku, the Sapphic, or the ghazal." He is right. The situation is absurd. Many will remember when, fifteen or so years back, the classical Persian ghazal seized the imaginations of American poets like Adrienne Rich and Jim Harrison and others. Fine work was done. But how could these poets resort to a kind of poetry so remote and alien, and not give at least equal attention to the only major kind of poetry invented in our own country and our own time. The blues are not only expressive, they are ours. All the more reason to begin writing them.

7. As I say, I have written no blues that I think good enough to publish, and I should add that I've written only a few and only in recent years. I wish I had been writing blues from the beginning, or at least that they had been a persisting formal element in my poetry. I have written many other kinds of song, why not the blues? And now I see—for the first time utterly clearly!—how I was inhibited by the cultural chauvinism of the literary community. This was not conscious in me; I have played and sung the blues, and have written and talked about them, for many, many years, without the least feeling of condescension. I have been scornful of writers and critics who could not or would not acknowledge the determinative place of Afroamerican music in our contemporary civilization. Yet I did not write blues. The whole apparatus of literary production in this country, publishers big and small, editors, magazines, critics, universities, etc., militated against the idea of writing blues, militated against the idea even occurring to me. Yet I do believe that what Cummings did with the sonnet, to take a conspicuous example, could be done with the blues, if one had a lifetime to give to it. Now of course it is too late for me. But not for others.

IN THAT SESSION

In the mind's house of heaven the great night never
Ends.
    All the brothers are there: Berigan, Bechet,
Russell, Hawkins, Dickenson, Hodges,
And Mary Lou and Lady Day
And so many others.
          And oh they play, they
   jam forever,
Shades of strange souls nevertheless caught together
In eternity and the blues.
       No need
To cut anyone any more, no fatigue
From the straights out front or the repetitive changes,
But only expressiveness,   warmth,
Each invention a purity, new without strangeness
In that session.
      Always they strained on earth
For this thing, skin and soul to merge, to disappear
In howling sound.
     God, but it would be worth
Dying, if it could be done,
   to be there with them and to hear,   to *hear*.

JAMES WRIGHT'S
COLLECTED PROSE

"Well, this is the only life I have. In many ways it's a snarled mess, but I like it."

Unexceptional words. Nevertheless, to friends of James Wright, including thousands who know him only through his poems, they carry great meaning, perhaps greater than anything else in his *Collected Prose*, which is very miscellaneous indeed.[1] They were said in an interview only a few weeks before Wright discovered he had incurable cancer. When he died, he was fifty-two years old.

So I have been thinking of him, the man, the poet, thinking especially of ways to characterize his imagination. I see how he moved further and further into acknowledged bafflement, a desert in which he prospected for moments of clear feeling. Clarity of feeling was his mode of understanding.

The difference between understanding and knowing: Schopenhauer, among all modern philosophers the loveliest mind, defined them both without recourse to the idea of rationalism. This would have appealed to Wright. Some of his clear moments came to him in poems, but not all by any means, and he was interested in whatever stimuli of intuition he could discover.

When *Homo erectus* became *Homo sapiens*, it was instantaneous. Suddenly the mind performed what the experts call "symboling." That is, it superimposed the symbol upon the datum, imagination upon perception, understanding upon knowledge, as when the first cave paintings were made. For millennia this mutation of mentality was a source of gratification, but now we begin to see the terror and pathos of it. *Homo sapiens* moving away from the beautiful animals, inventing culture. Simply and complexly at the same time, Wright lived in that instant.

Culture is the possibility of imagination, and hence engages the terror of the future. Nietzsche wrote: "Everything that has existed is eternal, the sea throws it back on the shore." This is part of the terror. Austin Farrer wrote: "The loneliness of personality in the universe weighs heavily upon us. To put it somewhat quaintly, it seems terribly improbable that we should exist." This is another part.

To find oases of clear feeling in the desert of improbability, Wright again and again risked quaintness. Sartre wrote: "What we call a feeling is merely the abstract unity and the meaning of discontinuous impressions." To set down discontinuous impressions, which in subjectivity are nevertheless not irrelated, and to chance folly in the hope of feeling and clarity, this is what Wright did. In the face of moralistic objectivism, the puritan element in modernity, he was not afraid to call a poem an "abstract unity." A poem is cultural; it is an act of symboling. It may be, alas, a quaintness.

But there are kinds of symbolism. We have been taught to think first of Laforgue, Hofmannsthal, Valéry, and of course T.S. Eliot; but this strand did not much appeal to Wright. He was closer to Georg Trakl, René Char, Cesar Vallejo, also to the Chinese classical masters, also to Robinson and Frost. He tried hard to avoid the forcing and the self-conscious allusiveness of heavy-handed emblematicism. Instead he was close to nature, especially to small things in nature, and he wanted them to come into his poems naturally and to assume their symbolic functions with a certain delicacy or shyness.

At the same time he was a workingman's son. Not once, I think, does he mention proletarian literature, yet I hear Steinbeck and Farrell in his poems as often as I hear Tu Fu. He took this for granted, particularly in the obsessive poems about Martin's Ferry, Ohio, and Minneapolis, his two absurd hometowns. He called himself a conservative, only half in jest. He was free to do so because he stood on ground which, however ugly, had been won for him (and for us) by great radicals, in the same way that the New Critics, whom Wright admired (he graduated from Kenyon College), were free to play with Kantian epistemological esthetics because Taine, Legouis and Cazamian, More, Parrington, Wilson, Burke, and others like them had done the dirty job of making writers accountable.

No doubt what I'm writing now is more a poem than a review, and in Wright's manner too, this gathering intensity of impressions. "Yeah, that's what you been doing for years now, foisting it off as some kinda knowledge." So speaks the Interlocutor. *Mea culpa.* The reason you become a tribal elder at age sixty is because just that many years are needed to acquire disillusion. Wright did not make it. But he was headed in that direction. The most frequent answer to questions in his last interview is, "I don't know."

Besides, even while poetry-as-composition-in-verse recedes toward cultural evanescence, poetry-as-a-mode-of-imagination engulfs all other literature—fiction, essays, editorials, whatever. A question of compensatory obsolescence, as when field artillery replaced the dinosaurs, etc. The real epic of our time is *The Rebel*, by A. Camus.

Wright called himself also "Horatian," by which he meant his belief in the poem as made; a thing, an object, possibly a container; definitely not an expression or transmittance. A poem is a system, "organic" or "mechanistic" as you will, these schematizations being no more accurate than the graphics of TV commercials; but systemic integrity is the poem's *sine qua non.* Craft is important. Yet Wright had little to say about it. Ultimately craft is personal, almost infinitely delicate, and learned in private and relentless failure, until it becomes like the *pratique* of Balinese dancing, inseparable from feeling, the content of centuries coalesced in the arch of a finger. And feeling, if it is clear, becomes value. And value, if it is real (i.e., in a real poem), becomes assimilated to the past and extrapolated from the past, as we do ourselves in our acts of going-beyond. Wright died every time he wrote a poem.

". . . the most difficultly courageous way of asserting the shape and meaning of one's own poetry and one's own life is to challenge and surpass those very traditions and masters whom one can honestly respect." That is an early formulation. Later he worked hard to make his prose simpler and more precise, and he inserted chunks of it into his books of poems, saying emphatically, however, that these were indeed prose, not "prose-poems." If he had lived longer, he would have written a remarkable work of prose, probably humorous. In his extreme seriousness he complained that his own poems were not funny enough, and he loved the comic masters, Cervantes and Dickens.

In Wright-as-he-hoped-to-be, laughter was the reverence paid to things as they are. Wright-as-he-was usually was not up to it. "It's possible through poetry, I hope, to contribute to the continuity of life, and also to surrender one's own egotism to the larger movement of things." Then after a pause he added: "It may not even be a hope."

He loved the present tense. In the fiction of an eternal present no conflict can be resolved. Reality is an impasse. Personality is the plasmodium of endurance, a scarecrow in January.

Robert Bly and Gary Snyder were two of Wright's closest literary friends; the three had quite similar poetic aims—very broadly, the evocation of meaning in the meaningless. But Bly is more shrill than Wright, more insistent and gullible, while Snyder often seems in his poems to be somewhere else. Wright was the most patient and intent. He called Trakl's poems, some of which he translated, "quiet places at the edge of a dark forest where one has to sit still for a long time and listen very carefully," and he hoped the words could apply to his own. But he still insisted that a poem is a made thing.

Wright's imagination is not mystical but conjectural; that is to say, doubtful. This is very important. He came to discard most of the doctrinal New Criticism he had absorbed in his youth, seeing its élitism and moral self-contradiction, though he continued to admire the poems of Ransom, Tate, Warren, etc. But he chose the American way of being meditative, disclaiming both prescriptive existentialism and the reconditery of orientalism, though he learned from both; and the American way is to lay ambush among impressions for those that will unite in natural, single, clear, and practical feeling—and all four adjectives are crucial. He is irrational but reasonable. He lives on danger and writes in the risk of folly. What can be more American than that?—granting America is a condition of nostalgia. Those who love American wisdom will find some of it in Wright's prose, but chiefly in his asides, not in the major aims and topics. Many of his essays, introductions, reviews, etc., have the air of being obligatory, as Wright would have affirmed, for the sense of obligation is the tax levied upon feeling by experience, and so do the interviews, which are rambling and often in the wrong direction. Wright did not know how to turn off an interviewer; but since the only poet who does know how is Peter Redgrove, I suppose we can't be hard on Wright. I believe my view here is effectively arguable, namely, that it is far more important to fix the greatness of Wright as at the same time one of our most representative and most commanding poets than to faint-praise his agreeable, occasionally illuminating criticism, which in fact is not original and not otherwise distinguished. His best pieces are those in appreciation of his favorites, Whitman, Trakl, Char, R.P. Warren, and others; but even in these what I value are the corroborations of what I already know about Wright himself, chiefly from reading his poems, though to some extent from letters and conversations.

He is there in his book, at any rate, as in all his books, standing a little remote now, inconsistent, serious, battered, cautiously alarmed, chuckling over the debris of disbelief around his feet, but still the modest hero of the myth we live by, a man who responds to American harshness and violence "with a huge effort of imagination," as he wrote of Whitman, "to be delicate, precise, sensitive"—and, I would add, honest. Delicacy, precision and sensitivity have to do with the poet's relationship to us; honesty with his relationship to himself. Most poets, including most well-known poets, never ask themselves if what they feel is true, in any of the senses of truth; such turning upon the self is too frightening; better to stick with the received or long-since-derived ideas. Adolescence is the seed-time of most minds. Wright demanded more of himself, and if his honesty left him very doubtful, it also left him very resolute.

NOTE

1. James Wright, *Collected Prose*, ed. Anne Wright (Ann Arbor: University of Michigan Press, 1983).

MYSTERY AND
EXPRESSIVENESS

The two kinds of expressiveness in art, sensual and conceptual, are separable from substance only in theory, in analysis; this is understood. And I no longer believe, as I once did, that theoretical and analytical discussion, whether public or inside one's head, is necessary to understanding. Blest are they who respond fully to poems, paintings, musical compositions, and so on, without thought; for thought is the only product of theory and analysis, which are exercises of the mind for their own sake, or for intellectual pleasure, and though many of us become addicted to them, they serve only a cognitive function and have little, if anything, to do with understanding.

Young people, when they read a poem or look at a painting, do not ask whether and how it is expressive, but only what it says, what it shows, what it means. This is as it should be. Contrary to the notion of certain sophisticated critics, what we ask of a work of art in ordinary, pragmatically verifiable experience is what it signifies. From the point of view of the artist and the spectator, that is, leaving the critic aside, if significance were nugatory, the compositional process would break down, as indeed we have seen with certain third- and fourth-generation abstract expressionists who ended up in one or another order of minimalism, complaining that they had no more "problems," by which they meant invented formal incompatibilities on the surface of the canvas, to solve. Every artist must have something to make art about.

To these ideas a corollary must be added: perhaps the greatest utility of theory and analysis is their indication of their own limits. No matter how far one may press an investigation of expressive means, no matter how near one may edge to "final knowledge," a cognitive ending or point of rest will never be reached. An effective line of poetry, for instance, will never disclose all the elements of its own prosody. Even the most elaborately programmed computer could never find them, which is to say that every line of poetry, in all its prosodic combinations, is unique. Thus mystery lies at the extreme of knowledge—at the end or at the center, depending on how you look at it. Those who pursue knowledge the furthest will see, not the mystery, for it is precisely hidden, but the inevitability of mystery, most clearly, though whether or not this vision is an aid to understanding I do not know. But the acknowledgment of mystery is at least salutary.

Expressiveness in art derives from the work's embodiment, the work's presence and actuality, as opposed to its substance, which was once called content, an unreliable term. Substance is meaning; expressiveness is means. Someone will say that the means are part of the meaning, and I agree, of course. But let's keep the discussion as simple as we can, granting that any analysis of a work, any wrenching apart of the whole, is already complex and abstract. Then what is meant by the two kinds of expressiveness? Conceptual expressiveness derives from abstract technique: in poetry from figures of speech and from imagery, both direct and metaphorical; in painting from composition; in music from tempo, dynamics, keys, modes, and anything that has to do with combining and contrasting tonal and rhythmical patterns; and so on. Sensual expressiveness derives from the medium or from—excuse the expression—concrete technique: in poetry from the sounds, rhythms, and other verbal manifestations; in painting from pigment and its liquifacient and fixative agents; in music from tones, which are frequencies of vibration, what some people call notes or distinctions of pitch; and so on. At any rate these are the best approximate definitions I can come up with at the moment. It will be seen that expressiveness, both kinds, is a function of what has been called either style or form at different times and places, for, contrary to much current belief, these terms have been used not only variably but interchangeably in the evolution of western criticism and esthetic philosophy; but here the emphasis is on the function, not on the static, achieved artifact in its inertness, which is how critics usually perceive a work of art. Expressiveness is an active quality, not a passive one.

But really I find myself embarrassed to be discussing such simple and rudimentary matters. I do so only because I so often come into contact with artists who do not discuss them or who are even unaware of them. Yet artists, as distinct from spectators, are the ones who need to be concerned. Not so much with conceptual expressiveness perhaps, because this is fairly steadily dealt with in workshops, whereas I have the impression that sensual expressiveness is not. Here, however, I am getting onto shaky ground. I do not know enough about painting, sculpture, film-making, architecture, etc., to generalize the degree or kind of self-scrutiny common among their practitioners and teachers. What I do know about are jazz and poetry.

Several times in recent years I have given a talk called something like "Mystery and Expressiveness in Jazz and Poetry," and I have thought about turning it into an essay, but have been stumped by the impossibility of representing some of the materials on paper: my "talk" consists in large part of playing tapes as well as reading poems. I begin my talk with the last recording of Billie Holiday, taken from a live television concert not long before she died. I wasn't lucky enough to see the original program, but I have several times seen a film of part of it. Holiday—her face a little worn, but still very beautiful—sits on a stool among some of her favorite musicians, Ben Webster, Lester Young, Henry Allen, and others, and her voice is much stronger, much less quavery, than it was on the last studio recordings she made. (To infer, as I have heard some people do, that she had been given a controlled dose of heroin by the producers of the program is unfair to them and to her, and is reductive with respect to the power of the music.) She sings a blues, nodding her head to the beat, smiling. She sings simply but with her superb sense of timing and phrasing intact. It is a somewhat slow blues, and the words are silly in some verses, quite meaningful in others. (This blues and other excerpts from the concert were issued by Columbia on an album entitled *The Sound of Jazz*, CS 8040, 1958.) At the end is a one-bar tag by Webster on tenor, and at the very end, just after the final beat but while the tone is still sounding, somebody moans. It is scarcely audible, but in my talk I play the final bars again with the volume turned up so that the audience can hear it easily. (The voice sounds to me like Vic Dickenson's, but that's a guess.) Then I ask the audience what this moan means.

And I have had dozens of improbable answers, everything from pain because the tenor tag ends on a fourth instead of the dominant, which is ridiculous, to joy, love, understanding, sympathy, sorrow, etc. When I say that the moan does not *mean* anything, that it is an involuntary response to a purely sensual experience, that it suggests deep feeling but no specifiable emotion, nothing that a literary label can be attached to, that the feeling expressed is of undifferentiated physical experience, like the sound a man might make upon hitting a tennis ball or waking with a hangover or experiencing orgasm or death, when I suggest these things, the people in the audience begin to feel uncomfortable, and they shift around in their seats and lift their hands to rub their noses or pat their hair. From the platform it looks like a little flutter or spasm passing through them. Have they been taken so far out of their own bodies that they cannot deal with sensuality as such any more?

After the blues by Holiday I play another by Joe Turner, recorded at a concert in 1967 when he was still at his best (*John Hammond's Spirituals to Swing 30th Anniversary Concert*, Columbia, G 30776, 1967). The tempo is slower this time, the words are in some verses more sorrowful, and in some passages Turner sings with a sob in his voice. In the middle, when the vocal leaves off for a while and an instrumental ad lib begins, there is a loud, high-pitched yell, "Wahoooo!"—I presume from Turner himself. At the end I ask my audience what this means, and again I am given the names of emotions, and a few people are likely to be quite insistent, even testy, about it. But am I wrong? Does a musical pitch *mean* anything in our minds? Let's say an E-flat coming after a D and accompanied by a diminished chord: does it *mean*? This is a question of vibrations-per-second striking against ear drums and other sensory components. Can this mean something in itself? No, meaning is always in part a product of mind; the precisely appropriate response to musical pitch is a physical one—horripilation, a writhing sensation in the spine or a wrenching in the gut, a wince, a scowl—and if in the process a groan or yell escapes, the fact that it is a vocalization does not make it a verbalization. Many people, apparently, don't know this distinction. Which perhaps is natural.

After the music I play tapes of sounds from nature, peepers in spring, wind in a spruce forest, wild geese passing overhead at night, and then tapes of manufactured sounds, a train whistle, the din of massive machinery; and in none of these cases can the audience make an authentic specification of meaning, which causes them to be even more uncomfortable. Yes, I do understand the temptation to say that the sound of the geese overhead in the darkness is the voice of God or one's ancestral spirits passing and calling, or that the train makes a "lonesome" sound. This is what primitive people have always done. But I think such people, whose lives were immediately and intimately connected with nature, knew what they were doing and did it consciously, the fantasizing and symbol-making, the superimposing of culture upon sensory data, and they kept clearly in mind the reality of their situation, their place. A goose is a goose is a supper. This double talk or double thought is just what mankind in a situation of contrived existence has lost the capacity for, in spite of all the high-powered attention that has been devoted to poetic ambiguity in our time. Of course we cannot be primitive. Perhaps it behooves us then to be realists, in which case we must be extremely wise and cautious in the choice of words to apply to the sound of the geese. (Writers know that adjectives always weaken the nouns to which they are attached, even when they are necessary. Modification entails diminution. The folk know it too, which is why our language in recent decades has shifted so far in the direction of adjectival nouns and compound nouns.) Yet we must talk, we must write poems; which means that we must put ourselves into relationships with other people that require explanation and description, something more than finger-pointing. What shall we say, that the sound of the geese is eerie and yet appropriate?—as the sound of ghosts might be? This in fact suggests the ghosts or God, and the geese are geese. Better to describe the effect produced, a nostalgia for the unknown that is, as we say, felt "in our bones" and transmuted immediately to tension in muscles and nerves. Better to talk only to those who have heard the geese themselves, those who respond in the same way you do, at least more or less. And this is what is meant by community.

How much we have lost verbally in our forced collectivization, which is the inflation, not to say exploitation, of community.

After the tapes I begin to read poetry, passages or whole poems in which the substance is either so foolish or so obscured that it becomes functionally irrelevant, especially in aural apprehension: things like John Lily's "Cupid and my Campaspe . . . ," a particularly turgid page from *Paradise Lost*, some vacuous Dryden, a spun-out commonplace from *The Prelude*, and so on, down to Swinburne, Pound, Duncan, Gary Snyder; it is not at all difficult to find such pieces even among contemporary poets whom we think of as utterly substance-oriented, lovely, musical, sonorous, swinging, or foamy, and meaningless, passages that will evoke a *frisson* from everyone in the audience who has ears to hear and nerve-endings to feel. This of course does not mean everyone, for some are, it seems, genetically unable to respond to poems, and many others, legions of others, have been turned off to poetic values by our schools and by the vocal dullness of much American poetry in the twentieth century. It takes more than a public lecture to reawaken them. Yet not much more perhaps. People have told me that my talk has helped them.

And at this point in the talk I scarcely need to say anything more: the point has been made by the examples. Expressiveness in art is not a function of substance. Not at all. Originality of thought and feeling, novelty of event, cogency of allusion, and all other elements of substance are, in the best sense of the word, literary; they are what poets *do*. The sensual and conceptual elements are, so to speak, what poets *are*: the conditioned and/or instinctive skill within which they exist. Expressiveness is what draws poets to poetry in the first place, and it is what older poets more and more return to as they consolidate and simplify their poetic vision. And the same holds in all the arts.

Does this mean a work can be done with no substance at all? At one time or another workers in all the arts have tried it, but I am certain it is impossible except in music. I believe that, speaking theoretically and analytically, a musical pitch is pure and has no meaning. I believe—though how can one be sure?—that my own musical ideas occur to me, when I am improvising, only as sequences of pitch, texture, and rhythm, with no literary or cultural attachments whatever. I am not a singer, and I care less for vocal music than for instrumental. Yet it is obviously true that much music, probably most music, does occur in what we may call a literary or cultural context. Practically speaking, pure music may be as impossible as pure art in general, pure expressiveness. Nevertheless music *tends toward purity*, and to my mind Schopenhauer was right when he suggested that the other arts aspire to the condition of music, except that I wish he had said "ought to aspire."

A great many artists from all times and places have attested that the inception of a work of art, its origin, its "inspiration," is an event of simultaneous, mutually reinforcing emergence of substance and its expressive means, both sensual and conceptual. This is particularly evident in the improvisatory art of the twentieth century, whether it be a solo by Cannonball Adderley or a circus by Peter Schuman's Bread and Puppet Theater.

The truth of course is that in this time we have many poems and other artworks that are inexpressive; it has become the norm. Composers and performers make music without much concern for its impact on the body of the auditor, and poets conventionally write prose, or at best poems radically tending toward prose. In architecture the concrete block has become a model, and in paint-ing we have super-realism on one hand and blank canvas on the other, equally inexpressive. In jazz the conservatories and work-shops have introduced an imitative academicism, finicality, and virtuosity that seem—at any rate to me—extraordinarily boring.

But I see counterindications too, artists who recognize that the attitudinal significance of pop culture, with its rock music and heavily metered greeting-card verse, is worth paying heed to. Young composers, like my friend William Duckworth, are not only acknowledging their roots in the blues, jazz, and rock—which are, and this is no overstatement, whatever the *New York Times* says, the classical music of America—but also showing that they understand their roots. (Not the case with Copland, Gershwin, and other composers of that generation.) And although much of the music composed during the past twenty-five years on syn-thesizer and tape, *la musique concrète*, seems to me artistically insincere, some is not, and the search for new expressive means with electronic instruments continues to be rather exciting. In jazz some musicians are using the voice primitively, i.e., instrumen-tally, and are using instruments more, rather than less, bluesily, i.e., outside the diatonic modes. Notice the increasing popularity of string quartets in jazz, and the skill of the performers on un-fretted string instruments that can be tuned easily to any scale and played in any mode. The performance of Thelonious Monk's piano pieces by the Kronos Quartet is a case in point; the quartet can *play* what Monk could only intimate on the piano. (But Paul Zukofsky's performances of rags, which are a legitimately pian-istic music, are no better than travesty.) In poetry I see many young people scouting the fringes of literature, both the conven-tional and the unexplored fringes, in search of ways to make their poems more sensual, more expressive. And painters like Susan Bush are finding quite new and expressive means in their graphic use of commonplace materials for effects of sensual immediacy. In sculpture Judith Brown is a good example.

At all events I think I perceive the closing of the time when one will hear of a literary work the criticism that "it is too well written," of a piece of music that it is "too sonorous" or "too mellifluous," or that any musical or literary or painterly qualities are "distract-ing." (I have heard all of these within the past three days.) The signs are not as clear as one might wish. They never are. But I suggest that works like the recordings of simple songs in the ear-lier Afroamerican tradition by Horace Parlan and Archie Shepp, in which—at least in the best of them—the musical expressiveness is new, moving, yet firmly integrated with substance, or like the novel *Luisa Domic*, by George Dennison, in which the writing is both gratifying in itself, to anyone with an ear for the possibilities of American speech, and thoroughly at one with the novel's remarkable substance and vision—I suggest that such works as these, and a good many others, do manifest a turning away from inexpressive formulaic virtuosity and a desire to meet the real needs of the human mind and spirit, which are perennial. But I do not wish to be misunderstood. Ray Carver has been called a "minimalist," a "writer of fragments," a "stylistic vacancy," etc. but to my mind he is none of these, and his best stories are expressively and substantially complete, trenchant, compelling, and in their way beautiful. Naturally Carver has accepted the limits of his verbal imagination, or rather he has partially accepted them while he continues to push against them. What else can any artist do? The artist who functions equally well in all conventions does not exist, and all expressive works—even the largest, e.g., *À la recherche du temps perdu*—can *be* expressive only within their own acknowledged frontiers.

Already what we must watch out for is the coming upon us of the *baroque nouveau*. In the main lines of every American art today we see powerful tendencies toward the pedantic, the establishmentarian and the hyperesthetic. In short, a new decadence. Without denying the appeal exerted on us by a less than responsible art, I believe we must reject it—as serious artists always have. But this isn't easy. In particular cases the artist will very often be hard-pressed even to decide what must be rejected, and how, and when. This tension is the source of expressiveness in our lives, or at least one source. Probably we need it in order to know how to be expressive in our work.

At the far end of expressiveness, or at its center, its point of impulsion, lies the mystery. The mystery is not cryptic, though some artists choose to believe it is and even derive from it, as cryptesthesiatically from "another source," their own artistic vision. If this works for them, then who objects? But for my part a distinction exists between the *cryptic* and the *labyrinthine*. The cryptic is a hiddenness associated with another order of perception, whether finite or infinite. It is totally outside my competence. But the labyrinthine is a hiddenness associated with human perception, our way of seeing; it is an obscurity of finite complications too distant, minute, and tangled for our finite discernment to clarify. No one will ever penetrate to the heart of the labyrinth. If my powers of analytical and theoretical intelligence are too weak, and if my capacities of imagination are too limited, to allow me a complete realization of the procedures of expressiveness, then I rejoice as much as anyone in what surpasses my understanding and in the wonderful fortuities, the instances of what-happens, that occur when I am putting together a work of art. This always has been and, as long as artists exist, always will be the greatest joy we have in our finite, contingent, and terrified lives.

AN EXPATIATION ON
THE COMBINING OF
WEATHERS AT
THIRTY-SEVENTH AND
INDIANA WHERE
THE SOUTHERN MORE
OR LESS CROSSES
THE DOG

Well, Ammons rolled the octaves slow
And the piano softened like butter in his hands,
And underward Catlett caught the beat
One sixteenth before the measure with a snip-snap touch on
    the snare
And a feathery brush on the cymbal, and Shapiro
Bowed the bass, half-glissing down past E-flat to A, to D,
And after a while
Berigan tested a limping figure low
In the cornet's baritone and raised it a third and then
    another
Until he was poised
On the always falling fulcrum of the blues,
And Bechet came in just as the phrase expired
And doubled it and inverted it
In a growl descending, the voice of the reed
Almost protesting, then to be made explicit
On the trombone as O'Brien took it
And raised it again, while Berigan stroked a high tone
Until it quavered and cried,
And Carruth achingly came on, the clarinet's most pure

High C-sharp, and he held it
Over the turn of the twelfth measure
And into the next verse with Bechet a fifth below rumbling
Upward on the back beat powerfully,
And O'Brien downward,
And Catlett press-rolling the slow beat now,
The old, old pattern of call and response unending,
And they felt the stir of the animal's soul in the cave,
And heard the animal's song,
Indefinable utterance, and saw
A hot flowing of the eternal, many-colored, essential plasm
As they leaned outward together, away from place, from
    time,
In one only person, which was the blues.

INSTANCES

What we disparagingly call taste is nevertheless at the bottom of everything we say about the arts. We strive for objectivity, but are bound in subjectivity. Both our bonds and our striving are important; we must recognize and study them; they are aspects of the human condition, or of our knowledge of the human condition—defining aspects that tell us what we are. At the same time, therefore, in any discussion of the arts it becomes crucial to isolate and scrutinize the individual sensibility, and to consider how it has been formed.

1. In the small farming community in western Connecticut where I grew up during the twenties and early thirties, jazz itself was not known, though the word was. What it stood for was something foreign, exotic, and certainly wicked. We were not cut off from the world, we had radios, we knew the pop tunes of the day, all those hymns to geography, "Stars Fell on Alabama," "Avalon," "The Sheik of Araby," "Moon over Miami," "Dardanella," "I'm Coming, Virginia," "Roses of Picardy," etc., which, although I was spellbound by almost all music, I considered preferable to the Hungarian rhapsodies and shrieking Rhenish operas my mother loved. I knew the words and melodies, I'm sure, of dozens of Tin Pan Alley songs. I can remember singing "Love Is Just around the Corner" when I was about ten or eleven, with scat interpolations in the manner of Armstrong; I can even remember most of the words today, though I haven't sung them once in the intervening fifty years.

But I never heard jazz as such until the one kid in town whose parents were rich enough to send him to private school came home at the end of term one spring with a few records that he played for me. I'm not certain, but I think this was in 1932. Nor do I remember clearly what the music was, though I still have an impression of records that sounded like early Ellington and Fletcher Henderson. Later I do remember distinctly the record of Goodman's "Stomping at the Savoy," played for me by the same friend, and that was in 1934. At that time I played the harmonica, penny whistle (flageolet), ocarina, ukelele, and violin, with all of which I practiced what I took to be jazz rhythms, breaks, intonations, etc., though I knew nothing of the blues or the jazz repertoire of that period.

Nevertheless I was surrounded by music. In church I sang and memorized the hymns favored by the Episcopalian congregation. I pumped the organ. In school we had singing every day, and an itinerant singing teacher once a week. We also listened regularly to the radio broadcasts for children conducted by Walter Damrosch; the teacher brought her own little AM radio, very tinny, and set it facing us on her desk, with the volume turned way up. When I was about twelve, I began attending the dances held at the town hall for the whole community. I have never seen or heard of such dances since then. Two bands played alternating sets all night long. One was a country band, though I don't remember that term being used, and the other played pop tunes for what was called ballroom dancing, fox trots and waltzes. The country band consisted essentially of a fiddler, a drummer, and a caller, sometimes augmented by a second fiddle, piano, banjo, accordion, etc. The other band was a sax, traps, and piano, occasionally with a violin or cornet added. (The head of the bass drum was always painted with a romantic scene, moonlight on water, for instance, with lovers drifting in a canoe and palm trees in the background.) We kids preferred the reels and square dances played by the country band, because these were a license for us to hurl one another about in a frenzy of emergent sexual athleticism. Yet sometimes we simply stood and watched the weathered farmers and stout farmwives, who danced with a dignity and grace we would never have suspected from seeing them in their everyday occupations. As for the ballroom dancing, we were awkward and shy. It was the fashion then among our immediate elders—the sixteen- and seventeen-year-olds and the young married couples of eighteen—for the woman to lay her head on her partner's shoulder with her arm around his neck while at the same time jutting out her rear end to get enough clearance for her feet to avoid being stepped on. It looked absurd but exciting. We wondered if we'd ever have the courage to get that close to anyone.

But the music was what fascinated me. Often I would stand below the rim of the stage to watch the musicians. I marveled at the fiddler's technique and his relentless pace, and I marveled too at the way the musicians of both bands worked together as if by instinct, for they rarely used scores or charts. I knew from listening to my friend's records that I was not hearing jazz, far from it, but I recognized certain jazz-like elements, and certain universal elements as well, and these were enough to set me going on all kinds of improvised fantasies. I became aware, though I could not have put it clearly into words, that from a very early time, from before my conscious memory, music had been the most important thing in my life, but also that this was wrong and shameful. My father was totally unmusical; he not only couldn't carry a tune, he couldn't distinguish any intervals of pitch whatever. Talk about tone-deafness, he was the all-time champ. Music was my mother's province. My father, of course, was a well-intentioned man and a rationalist, who would never have expressed open disapproval of anything as conventionally "good" as music; but in our household, as in so many others of that time, no doubt at all existed about which one was the authority-figure or which was to be emulated. It was a deeply sexist family. In the processed underlayers of my mind music became tainted with unworthiness and triviality, and my fascination became disreputable. So much the worse when my fascination turned to focus on jazz, the music that was socially and culturally contemptible almost everywhere. I became a secret jazz lover.

2. In those days the psychological testing and counseling of children, the whole apparatus of psychiatric awareness that we take for granted in our schools today, was unknown, and no one suspected that the secret jazz lover was secretly screwed up in general. I didn't suspect it myself. I knew I was "different" and "unhappy," and that my difference and unhappiness were considerably magnified in 1935 when my father lost his job and the family moved to Pleasantville, N.Y., which was as close to a family homestead as we possessed; my grandparents had settled in Pleasantville in 1910, when northern Westchester County was still a region of villages and farms. By 1935 my grandparents were dead, and Pleasantville, though still a village in many respects, was a good deal more suburban, more sophisticated, than our old home in Connecticut had been. I was miserable. I longed for the old home, and have longed for it ever since. I became "withdrawn" and my behavior, as I see in retrospect, was clearly phobic. But in my ignorance I adjusted as well as I could, the way children do.

For jazz I relied on the radio, which was not at all unusual in those years of the Depression. I had a huge battered fourth-hand "console" that stood next to my bed. Late at night, when I was supposed to be sleeping, I turned it on with the volume very low, and spun the dial until I picked up remote broadcasts of dance bands from hotels and clubs all over the country. Most of this was awful music, truly wretched, and I knew this; but I listened anyway. On Sundays I found programs of black gospel music or spirituals broadcast from churches in Harlem. On weekday afternoons I listened to "The Make-Believe Ballroom," a program in fifteen-minute segments of new releases by the pop bands of the day. Its DJ was Martin Block, who became a power in the music business by playing mostly junk but including enough serious Afroamerican music to make adolescent listeners think they were getting something authentic and valuable as well as fashionable. I would listen for hours to Glenn Miller and Sammy Kaye and their like in order to hear one new record by Ellington or Lunceford or even the Benny Goodman trio. Once—and I remember this with a wrenching in my stomach—Block put on a new release from Victor of a group headed by Mezz Mezzrow and Sidney Bechet. It was two sides of a ten-inch 78 called "Comin' On with the Come On," one of Mezzrow's experiments in recreating the ensemble improvisation of early jazz. I thought it was not just wonderful but the most compelling, moving music I'd ever heard. Yet after a minute Block cut it off. "How can they let such nasty stuff be recorded," he said, or words to that effect. In an instant he became my enemy for life, the prototypical racketeer of pop culture. But I continued to listen to "The Make-Believe Ballroom." It was all there was.

Well, not entirely. In 1938 Goodman conducted the first jazz concert in Carnegie Hall amid much controversy, for it was the first American jazz concert in a "legitimate" hall anywhere, and it was a whopping success. Appearances by Goodman, Dorsey, Miller, and others at the Paramount Theatre in Manhattan were causing riots. If only by sheer numbers, the young people of the United States were forcing jazz, or an abstracted, subdued version of it, into middle-class culture. (Three decades later the same thing would happen again with another variant of jazz called rock-n-roll, which was taken from the ghetto dives of southern cities where it had been performed for years by such people as Piano Red and Big Mama Thornton.) As jazz became more widely accepted, programs of the real thing, if sufficiently "smooth," were put on the air. I remember a weekly "sustaining" program called "The Chamber Music Society of Lower Basin Street," which had

Lena Horne singing the blues—singing them very well. I remember also a weekly program by the John Kirby band, and I think others, including the principal white "swing" bands, which had sponsored programs: Benny Goodman, Artie Shaw, the Casa Loma band, etc. Some fine musicians were sidemen in these bands, and usually they were featured once or twice in each program, though the vocalists, singers of "ballads," were more prominent. The single most affecting radio program I heard was a dramatization of Dorothy Baker's novel, *Young Man with a Horn*. I have no idea who produced this (Orson Welles?) or who the actors were, but the incidental music was furnished by the band from Nick's, and Bobby Hackett played the protagonist's cornet solos. It was extraordinary. I had tuned in to it by accident but not long after it had begun, and I listened with something like reverence. I think in my ears the music was, in fact, sanctified.

At some point, I don't quite know when, I began going into the city on my own. I would head first for the Commodore Record Shop on 42nd Street, a block or two from Grand Central Terminal. It was a crowded, dusty, disorderly place, packed with records, almost a temple. Sometimes I saw people whom I recognized as musicians. Milton Gabler, the proprietor, ran a small recording company that issued records on the Commodore label, and I remember as if it were yesterday how rich I felt when I bought my first of his recordings—they were expensive—which was the double twelve-inch recording—four big sides—of "A Good Man Is Hard to Find," with Pee Wee Russell, Joe Marsala, Muggsy Spanier, Brad Gowans, Jess Stacey, George Wettling, and a number of other splendid musicians. I bought the records even though I had no machine to play them on. Later, when I got a phonograph, I played them until they became so scratchy that the music was almost gone. I still think Russell's first solo on that record is among his best work.

At some point also I finally made it to Nick's in the Village on Sheridan Square. I didn't go often, I didn't have the means; but I was there perhaps a dozen times before it folded. I could pass for twenty-one when I was sixteen, which was good for my interest in jazz and very bad for my interest in booze. Once I talked to Russell, or talked at him; he didn't say much. There was no reason why he should. Mainly I remember the smoky air, the tough, rat-faced waiters, and the band: Gowans walking back and forth along the front of the stand, waving his valve trombone imperiously; Russell with his face incredibly squinched when he took his solos; Hackett looking almost like a boy. The music wasn't always great, but it was free, genuinely expressive. It made an appeal to me that was irresistible, and had something to do with shaping my taste in music, in poetry, and in everything.

I don't mean I didn't go uptown to the swing joints along 52nd Street or the Roseland or the Apollo, etc. That came a year or two later. Like many others, I had memorized Lester Young's solo on "Lady Be Good," which was issued on record in 1936, and I cherished my experiences with Ellington, Erskine Hawkins, Andy Kirk, and the other famous black bands of the era. But when a jump tune degenerated into riffing—and as time went on this happened more and more often—I got bored. I wanted invention, not repetition; music, not blunt pounding. The lindy-hoppers were about as interesting as football players to me, i.e., not at all. I sought music that was inseparable in its expressiveness, with tonal and musical qualities equally important. For this reason I came to believe, for instance, that Ben Webster was a better tenorman, if only by an iota, than Lester Young, though in my generation it was, and is, heresy to say so. And Sidney Bechet remains for me the prototypical jazz musician par excellence. Not that Archie Shepp can't do ten times more with a soprano sax than Bechet could do, and I appreciate this, I know its importance; but I like Shepp best when he seems to me to be working in a direct evolutionary line, however distantly, from Bechet. I have long felt and often said that anyone who cannot hear Scott Joplin in John Coltrane is missing an essential ingredient.

3. I went to college, I served in the army, I entered graduate school, I began paying serious attention to writing, which had been another of my main interests from childhood on, though except in journalism it hadn't received much encouragement. I drifted, in other words, wherever chance and the exigencies of the times took me. Often I had no opportunity to hear jazz for long periods, and no one to talk with about it. In my undergraduate years at Chapel Hill, I knew only one other student who shared my intensity of feeling about jazz, Brad McCuen, who later became a prominent executive in the recording business; but at school we belonged to different groups and never became close friends. In the army I met no one who took jazz seriously, and I remember only one important listening experience. One hot night I was hanging out in the rather rudimentary eleventh-century Italian castle that my outfit (the 455th Heavy Bombardment Group, 15th AAF) used for a headquarters. Someone was playing V-disks on

the PA. Most of these specially issued records were by pop vocalists, the usual wartime sentimentality and nostalgia. But then
an almost literally electrifying blast came from the loudspeakers,
and it was Woody Herman's "Apple Honey," with the most remarkable trombone solo I'd heard up till that time. (Only a good while
later did I learn it was by Bill Harris, who went on, of course, to do
many other fine things.) When I got out of the army in October
1945, I went down to Nick's as soon as I could. But it wasn't the
same. I was never so worn out in my life, and everyone else seemed
tired too.

In Chicago, when I entered the university in March the next
year, I began to hear jazz again, and I met two friends, Clinton
Goree and Robert A. Park (known as Andy), who were as devoted
to jazz as I was and who were more knowledgeable. We bought
records, went to the clubs, spent hours in listening and discussing. Our hangout was the Bee Hive on 55th Street, a bar with a
bandstand, no better than others in that seamy neighborhood.
I met Don Ewell when he was working there, and through him
met other musicians in Chicago, Darnell Howard, Baby Dodds,
Muggsy Spanier, the Yanceys, some of the white musicians from
the 1930s who had stayed in the city, Floyd O'Brien, Jimmy
McPartland, Floyd Bean, etc. On the Near North Side was Jazz,
Ltd., a club owned by a clarinet player, I've forgotten his name; he
always played along with the hired musicians, and he was not
great. To judge by his expression he wasn't enjoying himself much
either, a feeling many amateur musicians will recognize. Jazz,
Ltd., featured primarily the new Dixielanders or Revivalists, bands
like that of Doc Evans. But sometimes better musicians appeared.
I heard Bechet there more than once. As much as I remember Bechet, I remember also the way Danny Alvin, in his bright bow tie
and smoking a pipe, backed Bechet on the drums, very quietly
but firmly and sympathetically, while he watched the older musician with rapt attention. Bechet himself seemed annoyed with the
other musicians, the management, the customers, practically
everyone. I couldn't blame him. Not long afterward he went to live
permanently in France.

I recall other isolated occasions, like hearing Erroll Garner at a
club in the Loop on a Sunday afternoon, probably about 1948,
and a band with Pee Wee Russell in it, I think at the same place
and on another Sunday. Russell was so drunk he could scarcely
stand; he played one or two notes for each four bars, drawing
them out as long as his breath would let him. He was far gone in

alcoholism, and I was dismayed; I would not have been able to guess that much of his best work still lay ahead of him. At a club far out on the West Side I heard George Brunies with a band of local stalwarts, perhaps in 1949 or 1950. In lofts along one block on South Wabash I spent hours at a stretch listening to used 78s that you could buy for a dime. Dingy rooms with high irregular stacks of records, like the broken columns of a Roman ruin. In those days jukeboxes could play only one side of a record; often one's searches were rewarded with a record utterly worn out on one side, the popular side, with something first-rate in mint condition on the flip side. Clint, Andy, and I haunted those places. On Wells Street, Jackson Boulevard, and other streets in that neighborhood, I heard a lot of pre-rock rhythm-and-blues, singers like Big Bill Broonzy, and also various bop groups, inept imitators usually, who did not help me to understand what had happened in the bop revolution while I was in the army. In 1952 when I moved to New York, I was myself so far gone in alcoholic addiction and psychogenic breakdown that I was disqualified in almost every respect, including that of intelligent listening. One of the few good things ensuing from my year and a half in New York was a Selmer Paris clarinet, which I bought, one afternoon when I was half-loaded, at Schirmer's, paying a good deal more for it than I could afford. But I still own that instrument, and it's a fine one.

My next twenty-five years were lived first in total seclusion and later in only very gradually diminishing remoteness and isolation. I had plenty of time to think about music, to listen to my old records and the few but precious new ones—LPs now—that I could afford to buy through the mail. Eventually, i.e., about five years ago, I acquired a tape deck and could tape pieces from my friends' collections and from the radio. In northern Vermont I met people who were, like me, amateur musicians and close to jazz, such as John Engels and David Budbill, and through letters I came eventually to know still others at a distance, people like Hank O'Neal and Brad Morrow, who have been immensely helpful to me. And I became friends with musicians who were, and are, extremely knowledgeable about music in general, especially the poet and composer Theodore Enslin and the composer William Duckworth. Strange as it may seem, since jazz is by and large a social, public art and most people who write about it are widely traveled—our emphasis on the compositional aspects of improvisation should never make us forget that jazz musicians are performers too and are affected by the advantages and disadvantages of their public roles—strange as it may seem, then, whatever value the essays in this book may have derives not from my youth, when I heard jazz in "live" performances, but from my middle years of reflection, solitary practicing, and listening over and over again to a comparatively limited selection of records.

One should pay tribute to the people who have given us intelligent jazz programs on the radio. I'm sure many, many who have had readier access to live jazz than I've had will nevertheless agree that the good DJs have been tremendously helpful and influential. Back in the 1950s, when I was totally immobilized, the jazz program conducted on station WBAI in New York by Nat Hentoff and Gunther Schuller gave me many ideas, many experiences of close listening. Later in Vermont Bill Barton was, and still is, a remarkably well-informed commentator on jazz of all periods; his programs were a source of much help to me when I lived there, and when I go back on visits I make a point of listening to him. In central New York I listened to Leo Rayhill, who has a daily program on WCNY in Syracuse. Rayhill is more conservative than Barton when it comes to jazz of the 1980s, but his judgment is acute in other respects, and I learned much from him. Where I am living now I cannot pull in clear signals from any stations that broadcast jazz. This is a real hardship. As for the network jazz programs on the national public radio, conducted by Marian McPartland, Billy Taylor, Joe Williams, and others, I find them sometimes useful but more often slick and hokey, at least in comparison with the best locally originated programs. Many local DJs do their work out of sheer devotion to jazz, and are paid badly for it if at all. They deserve our gratitude and praise.

People have criticized my writing about literature for its eclecticism, its lack of a systematic, or what I would call ideological, view. The same criticism applies to these essays. Like poetry, jazz is where you find it. Schools and movements mean nothing, or at least next to nothing; intensive and informed listening means everything. The great individuals are the great artists, Coleman Hawkins, Bunny Berigan, Dinah Washington, Mary Lou Williams, Vic Dickenson, Ornette Coleman, Sonny Rollins—but there are scores of them, perhaps hundreds in the whole history of jazz, which as an art has fostered independent thought and feeling more than any other in our time. In our necessary system of cultural economy many great ones are inevitably forgotten, musicians from every time and persuasion, people like Ike Quebec, Jimmy Giuffre, Frankie Newton, Ike Rodgers, Charlie Shavers, Lil

Green, Skip James, Steve Jordan—the list is long. Yet I know the work of these people. So do a few others. The main thing, in jazz as in all the arts, is first to care, then to know, and finally to appreciate, i.e., to avoid and combat musicology and other such forms of pedantic historicism like the plague. To this main thing I have given a large part of my life, and I am glad of it.

LETTER TO MAXINE SULLIVAN

Just when I imagined I had conquered
nostalgia so odious, had conquered Vermont and the half-
   dozen good years there,
here you come singing "A Cottage for Sale," which is a better
   than average song as a matter of fact, though that's
not saying much and it's been lost to my memory for years
   and years,
but you always had good taste, meaning the same as mine.
Oh Maxine, how screwed up everything is.
Your voice in 1983 is not altogether what it was in 1943,
nor are the Swedish All Stars up to the standard of John
   Kirby, Russ Procope, Buster Bailey, Charlie Shavers, Billy
   Kyle, and—but who was on drums? Ben Thigpen?
   Shadow Wilson?—
the names, names, lovely old names calling to me always
   through echoing dark; no, nostalgia will never be
   conquered—
yet your singing is as passionate as ever, evinced in these
   exact little accents and slurs and hesitations, the
   marvelous stop-time measures, the *languets* of song,
so that I am overcome by your musical excellence and also by
   anger and sorrow because everyone
hoo-hahs so outrageously over Ella Fitzgerald, the eternal
   bobby-soxer (and millionaire).
You, a black woman singing a white Tin Pan Alley tune in
   Sweden about my home back in Vermont,
and I in Syracuse, where the jasmine has no scent—
feelings and values scattering as the death-colored leaves
   scatter on this windy day.
Maxine, I cling to you, I am your spectral lover, both of us
   crumbling now, but our soul-dust mingling nevertheless

in the endless communion of song, and I hope, I believe,
   that you have striven, as I have,
beyond the brute moments of nostalgia,
into the timelessness of music,
and that you have someone with you, as I have Cindy.

SMITH

Anyone who wishes to write about the important contributors to jazz, especially in the early period, faces an immediate embarrassment: what to do with their names. In a good many cases the names pinned on them, or which they pinned on themselves, were originally chosen for reasons of press agentry, a vulgar press agentry at that, drawing on the sexual meanings implicit from the beginning in the word "jazz." One thinks of Jelly Roll Morton, Trixie Smith, Hot Lips Page, Chippie Hill, and many others. There were more legitimate nicknames too, like Fats Waller, Red Allen, Bix Beiderbecke, and of course there was the fake nobility, King Oliver, Duke Ellington, Count Basie, as well as hundreds, if not thousands from Jimmy Blanton to Charlie Mingus, who have been known by their diminutives. And what shall we say of that truly splendid artist, Cootie Williams? It worked, of course, this press agentry. To millions of fans all around the world these very extraordinary people have been known by their ridiculous trade names, which have been a conspicuous part of the hokum generated about jazz for years. Almost from its beginning jazz has been deeply infiltrated by show business, a fact which those of us who have taken the art seriously have always deplored. Naturally we don't want academic manners either; but when, in the midst of the most serious consideration we have had so far of the work of Ferdinand Morton, by a critic whose style is anything but frivolous, we find that great musician called, abruptly and blatantly, "Jelly," we can't help being taken aback. It's a small matter, granted. Yet forms and usages do have a certain secondary importance.

In the case of musicians who were men the embarrassment is easily enough surmounted. We refer to them by their surnames. But the musicians who were women present a greater difficulty. Bessie Smith, for instance. Or rather, not "for instance" but as a primary focus of attention, since she is both the reason for this review and one of the supreme artists in all American music. It happens that her name is not a diminutive, at least not legally; she was christened Bessie, not Elizabeth. Yet Bessie certainly sounds like a diminutive. Legalism aside, it *is* a diminutive. And it is what virtually all writers, from the pop journalists of *Variety* and *Down Beat* to the most serious critics, call her. For my part, however, I cannot separate this usage from a most sorry sort of condescension, a condescension not only toward art—would we call Mozart "Wolferl" (as his cousin did) or George Eliot "Georgie" (as I'm sure no one did)?—but also toward race and toward sex; and here, obviously, the problem of usage becomes more than a matter of form. Should we call her then, in the manner of some reviewers dealing with female poets, by both her names: Bessie Smith? That is awkward and soon becomes stilted in repetition. Should we call her Miss Smith, in the fashion of twenty years ago? Worse yet, quite out of the question. Should we call her simply Smith? This, I believe, is what my friends in the movement for women's liberation would prefer, which in itself might be a good enough reason for choosing it. In addition we have a precedent in the custom of referring to other outstanding women of the past by their surnames alone, especially women in the public arts: Duse, Schumann-Heink, Duncan. Yet "Smith" sounds in my ear with an unfortunate clunk. There is condescension attached to it, too, I think, and perhaps downright discourtesy—she herself would have thought so—if only because the name is so common. There are at least a dozen other Smiths who have been prominent in jazz alone: Pinetop, Stuff, Clara, Buster, Joe, Jabbo, Mamie, Willie the Lion, etc. Is there no way out? We can't rename her. (Legally her name was Mrs. Gee!) I only know that if I had found myself in the presence of that genius I . . . well, I would probably have stammered and said nothing. But certainly I would never have called her Bessie; I can't imagine that. And if I wouldn't have done it then, I won't now.

I shall call her Smith, in the expectation that time will wear off the strangeness of it. And in fact the name in isolation, now as I look at it, already begins to seem more fitting. Here was this black woman in the midst of an alien culture, a dark-complected woman who preferred that darkness both for herself and others—"I ain't no high yaller," she sang in one of her most famous blues—here she was, not only surviving but triumphing, and she did it by rejecting that alien culture and turning to her own people, or rather by staying with them and never leaving them. In them she found a culture rich enough for what she wanted to do. (She reminds us of how little a real artist needs for her sources.) True, she occasionally performed for white audiences, but not often and never in a spirit of parasitism; there was nothing in Smith's career to correspond with Ellington at the Cotton Club or Armstrong at the Paramount. Her own people in their poverty and minority were nevertheless rich enough and numerous enough to nourish her in full measure, both as an artist and as a person. Forty years before the slogans of black liberation were invented Smith was proud of her own and her people's blackness; she said so consistently and publicly. Essentially she was a tent-show performer all her life, though she played often in urban theaters. She took the country blues, in the purity of its lamentation and bitterness, and transformed it into an urban art, retaining the power of its origins within its newly sophisticated meanings; and that new sophistication, as we should expect from studying the evolution of the other arts, consisted chiefly of irony; racial and sexual irony, or rather the two intertwined and felt together so singly that they cannot be separated. Smith was a terrifically sexual woman, to such an extent that her heterosexuality spilled over into bisexuality with a naturalness that seems inevitable and perfectly unobjectionable, so that in some ways she anticipated elements of the women's revolution as well as of the black revolution. In her extraordinary touring shows she surrounded herself with a troupe of young black women, and transported them in her private railway car back and forth across the country, reveling in that powerful female atmosphere. Her singing was impelled in every tone and timbre, as a moment's listening will tell, by the power and pathos of all mankind's undifferentiated lust. Yet the power and pathos were always shaped—and limited and controlled—by irony. Smith triumphed, in other words, because she was an artist and a genius, because in the singleness of her musical imagination she could reject the elements of her condition that were not useful to her—the very elements that drove politically oriented activists of the time into desperation and exile—while the rest, the useful parts of her experience, were perfectly absorbed and transmuted. And perhaps the components of that irony which defined her art and life may be signalized after all in a very meaningful way under the rubric of the name that was put onto her, Smith, the commonest—one almost wishes to say the ugliest—name in the registry of her Anglo-Saxon oppressors.

This much is easy. Smith was an artist; she survived and triumphed as an artist. But beyond this we know very little about the precise factors that engendered her art; and unfortunately her newest biographer, Chris Albertson, does not help us to find them. Albertson's life of Smith is merely that, an uncritical biography which deals with the artist as if she were no more than a popular entertainer. It skips quickly over her first twenty-five years, the period about which we should particularly like to know more, and then gives us a year-by-year march through the remainder of her life from about 1922, when she first became prominent, to 1937, when she died in consequence of a crack-up on the highway near Clarksdale, Mississippi. It is a somewhat dull chronicle of engagements, tours, recording sessions, associations with managers and booking agents, earnings and losses, newspaper reviews, etc., together with an account of her personal affairs. The latter is a tawdry enough account at times, tawdry and tragic. Smith was, as she said herself, a gin-head (though she preferred moonshine when she could get it), and she was also, as she did not say, an artist. We know the type; we have read scores of similar accounts: debauches, despairs, jealousies, fights, repentances, and so on. It is not an edifying record, but I suppose we have to have it. Albertson's excuse for his labors is that the record has been clouded heretofore, partly through neglect, partly through the ineptness of enthusiastic but unscholarly chroniclers; and this is true. Albertson's research has helped to set straight the record. He has, for instance, sought out and interviewed Smith's adopted son, Jack Gee, Jr., who had been lost to sight for many years. He has also turned up additional evidence concerning Smith's death, though not enough to put an end to the controversy, one way or the other, over whether or not she died as a result of being turned away from a white hospital in Clarksdale. But nowhere in Albertson's book do we find any account of Smith as a working artist. We know she worked hard, she sang as often as she could, she rehearsed, she had close associations with many other musicians, she gave careful consideration to the writing of her own songs, which were among the best she recorded; but we do not know *how* she worked. Albertson pays no attention to this at all, which is astonishing. It is inconceivable, for instance, that Smith did not talk about the work she was pursuing with such intensity; yet there is no record. We know, because it is perfectly evident in her recordings, that she lived *in* and *for* her art; the rest was necessary misery. Not only was her singing, which meant for her, as their playing does for all real jazz musicians, an act of creation as well as of performance, her great joy, it was her repeated moment of being, the escape from history, society, biology—from all determinants—into the pure realm of creative existence. A biography which omits that life is hardly a biography at all.

Albertson's failure is the more surprising because we have enjoyed a considerable flowering of serious jazz criticism in the past decade, from such critics as André Hodeir, Martin Williams, and Gunther Schuller. As far as I know, Schuller's *Early Jazz*, published five years ago, is the best-informed and most thorough work of jazz criticism thus far.[1] Schuller's credentials are impeccable; as a composer and teacher he has achieved distinction, and his devotion to jazz has been evident for years. (The radio program conducted by Schuller and Nat Hentoff nearly twenty years ago in New York was one of the best jazz programs I ever heard.) In musical terms his exegesis of what actually lies in the important recorded performances of early jazz is often astonishingly revealing. It is just what we who began to love jazz thirty-five years ago wanted but could never find. I began listening to Smith's records at about the time she died, and I have been listening to them with great regularity and concentration ever since, but I heard new things in them when I listened with Schuller's textual commentaries and notated examples in hand. This is explication, the New Criticism of jazz, at its best. Schuller ends his section on Smith with these words:

> Bessie Smith was one of the great tragic figures, not only of jazz, but of her period, and she more than any other expressed the hopes and sorrows of her generation of jazz musicians. If that were all, we would have reason enough to eulogize her. But Bessie Smith was a supreme artist, and as such [she] transcends the particulars of life that informed [her] art.

This was published five years ago, and it should have determined everything written about Smith thereafter.

Yet there is a limit to what purely musical criticism can tell us. Jazz, like the other arts, derives from three sources: the folk tradition, the individual personality, and the professional *milieu*. A study of interaction among these three sources should be the main purpose of any biographer who writes about an artist. In

Smith's case the sources can be equated with the country blues tradition, which was already widespread in the south during her girlhood in Chattanooga and which has continued its own slow, almost underground evolution until the present day; with her own complex and tragic vision, as manifested in the timbre, tonality, and phrasing of her magnificent voice; and with the requirements of her role as a performer, in some part the requirements of her relationship to fellow serious musicians, like Armstrong, Joe Smith, Charlie Green, and Fletcher Henderson, and in larger part the requirements of the entertainment industry in general. It is true that Smith was, by all accounts, a fine theatrical performer; she could dance and tell jokes as well as sing, and she is said to have taken complete charge of the theater when she was on stage. Perhaps we can say that her success during her lifetime was chiefly owing to this skill as an entertainer. But the success of her records in the years since then can be owing to nothing but her art. And there is simply no doubt that she was, and is, the best blues singer, and one of the two or three best jazz singers, of all time. Any comparison of her records with those of her contemporary rivals, Clara Smith or Mamie Smith (no relations) or even Ida Cox, or with those of country male blues singers then or since, shows her great superiority, not only in her natively magnificent voice, but also in her ability to bend and slur the notes of her song with exact intonation, to propel syntax against meter, and to shape and sustain a whole performance with musical and emotional consistency. Her influence, together with Armstrong's, is felt as a dominant factor in the evolution of jazz through the crucial period of the 1930s. If we take the common and simplified theory that jazz was an amalgam of earlier forms, especially ragtime, with blues feeling and the "blues scale," then Smith epitomizes the latter influence, though this is not to say that the blues wasn't an extremely widespread phenomenon rooted in the cultural antecedents of all black people. Of course we can never find the exact springs of any genius, neither Smith's nor another's. But there are questions we can ask. How did she respond to the folk tradition in her youth? What did she learn precisely from Rainey and other older singers? What did she learn from ragtime and early jazz? Beyond her rich and powerful voice, which is always dwelt on by the critics, what about her ear, in both the musician's and the poet's senses?—for certainly in her inflection of the vernacular and in her own writing she was remarkably responsive to her people's speech. Above all what artistic values did she hold in view, as distinct from theatrical values, during her progress toward her best work in the years from 1925 to 1929? These and similar questions, instead of her fights and scandals, are the topics to which Smith's future biographers must address themselves if they wish to do justice to her and to us.

NOTE

1. Gunther Schuller, *Early Jazz: Its Roots and Musical Development* (New York, 1968). This is the first volume, extending to about 1930, of a projected critical history of all Afroamerican music.

TO ALL HUMAN
CONSCIOUSNESS THE
CLANDESTINE IS BASAL

Recently I reread *Middlemarch*, by George Eliot. It is a peculiar literary performance. The term "novel" seems almost not to apply, though of course that's what it is. Consider, however. It cannot be called a social novel because, except for one minor confrontation between Mr. Brooke and a drunken cottager, which Eliot threw in as a sop to her conscience and as a way to show the impingement of the Reform Bill and machine-wrecking on the landed classes, the whole underpinning of social England in 1830 is omitted. It cannot be called a psychological novel because all the principals, including the supposed heroine, Dorothea, are stereotypes, and moreover were stereotypes when Eliot was writing, figures abstracted from Fielding, Austen, Thackeray, and who knows how many other generalized prior sources. It cannot be called a novel of manners because no event in the novel, except perhaps the reading of old Featherstone's will, is properly a public occasion; everything proceeds by successive, often adventitious confrontations between two individuals, who are usually in a condition of para-normality. It cannot be called a philosophical novel because—well, it just isn't. Eliot was writing in a flush philosophical time, the time of Mill, Darwin, Spencer, to mention only the English, and she could have written, she was altogether capable of writing, a philosophical novel, that is, a novel of ideas; but the book contains hardly a single serious intellectual discussion, not even the encounters between Ladislaw and Dorothea in Rome, which show us only a pretentious young man instructing an eager but rather silly young woman.

In fact not one principal is an interesting person. Dorothea is serious and ambitious to do good works, at least in her own mind she is, but no one could be as credulous as she during the "courtship" of Mr. Casaubon. I know that many people, perhaps especially women, will quarrel with this and say that most women in 1830 in England not only could be but were exactly this credulous, to which I can only reply that Dorothea by deliberate intellectual choice married outside the conventions of her class and the wishes of her family, and it seems to me that if she had enough brains to do this she should have had enough to see through Casaubon. Maybe not. But I detect in Dorothea's actions, both in this and in other parts of the novel, a considerable degree of forcing—Eliot's need for the purposes of the novel to make Dorothea intelligent and stupid at the same time, which is not sufficiently accounted for *in the novel* by either the historical role of women or the eccentricity of Dorothea's mind and character. After she is married, Dorothea is said to look "with unbiassed comparison and healthy sense at probabilities," meaning the probabilities of Casaubon's personality, and why had she not possessed these same *natural* capacities a year earlier? As for Casaubon himself, he is a doddering scholastic hangover. Dorothea's sister Celia is a flittery twit, and her husband Sir James is an immense masculine null. Mr. Brooke is a ditherer, but rarely dithers enough to be amusing. Fred is Mickey Rooney. Lydgate is a man of hope, as foolish and irresolute as all such men. Rosamund is a twittery flit, complicated in an uninteresting way by her selfishness. And so on. The only person who attracts me is Caleb Garth, the man of good sense and loving concern, whose attitudes as a farmer, though they probably have led to exactly the ecological woes we are experiencing now, were at least pure and well-intentioned. But Garth, though in a curious way he holds the novel together, can hardly be called a principal character.

Usually the novel is said to be a study in marriage and a precursor of feminist consciousness. But why a precursor? Eliot herself had read Mill's essay on the slavery of women and a good deal other such material, and she was willing to live in love but without marriage in her own life. Why doesn't someone in *Middlemarch*, almost anyone, do the same? The only unwedded person at the end is Parson Fairbrother, as insipid a whist-playing clergyman as you'd care to meet, and even in his case we are led to infer that his bachelorhood is his bad luck. Did Eliot know what she was doing?

She did. She was doing the best she could, and the things I have said about the novel so far are conscious exaggerations, for the sake of argument. Without retracting them, I still can and do agree that *in some minor sense* the novel is social, psychological, a discussion of manners and ideas, etc. But none of this—I repeat, none—is enough to account for the power of the book, for the fact that it remains on our reading lists and the further fact that people like me take it down from the shelf and reread it three or four times in as many decades. *Middlemarch* is not only an appealing but a compelling book, and the reasons why, let us give thanks, are mysterious.

Yet the mystery is approachable. The "march" in *Middlemarch* is of course the now obsolete word for a political division of land, usually a border region, the territory ruled by a marquis (or marchioness). The village, in other words, is in the middle of an unspecified but politically bounded region, and Eliot was quite aware of the importance of a political attitude to understanding her story. Did she know how far this political implication extends, even into metaphysics? I doubt it. But certainly she knew the other meaning of "march," "a measured and regular advance," and that thus her village is not only in the middle of extent but in the middle of duration. It is the fantasized locus of all human space and time, the *civitas mundi.* In creating it, Eliot was doing something quite un-Victorian, even un-English, far exceeding, it seems to me, the English penchant for calculated allegory from *The Faerie Queene* to *Pilgrim's Progress* to *Vanity Fair,* all of which she knew well; Eliot was doing something which exceeded even her own realizations. At least this seems likely to me, even though I cannot tell how to guess the limits of her imagination. Neither can anyone else. We may only—but legitimately—infer from the text that the author's awareness was less than her achievement, as we do, for instance, in the case of *Tristan und Iseult* or *Aladdin. Middlemarch* reminds me of *The Castle* and *The Plague* more than of anything in English literature, either before or after. A crucial point is that Eliot's intelligence was not only great but instinctively continental, in which she resembles her contemporary Robert Browning, though with obviously different consequences.

The principal persons in *Middlemarch* are ineffective because they cannot be anything else. They are Everyman and Everywoman, acting in a plot that is almost entirely circumstantial, not topical—a kind of trap. Their political fate is ineffectuality, just as their existence is an accident. This is more than Eliot intended. But in the same way that we say of a modern poet that his or her poem means more than was put into it, or that the meaning hovers, so to speak, over the actual words and figures, Eliot's novel is greater than she conceived, and its full meaning, its ultimate appeal to us, slips into it, as into her consciousness, clandestinely. Is this not the case with all truly great works of the imagination? No computer could be programmed sensitively enough to select all the minute fortuities of tone, syntax, and diction that make such works persist centrally in our own consciousness. We know only that we are moved in ways and degrees that are unexplainable by reference to the works themselves, much less to the lives of their authors.

Nevertheless, perhaps a couple of quotes will be helpful. Here is a paragraph from the opening of part III of *The Plague*, by Albert Camus:

It was at this time that a high wind rose and blew for several days through the plague-stricken city. Wind is particularly dreaded by the inhabitants of Oran, since the plateau on which the town is built presents no natural obstacle, and it can sweep our streets with unimpeded violence. During the months when not a drop of rain had refreshed the town, a gray crust had formed on everything, and this flaked off under the wind, disintegrating into dust-clouds. What with the dust and scraps of paper whirled against peoples' legs, the streets grew emptier. Those few who went out could be seen hurrying along, bent forward, with handkerchiefs or their hands pressed to their mouths. At nightfall, instead of the usual throng of people, each trying to prolong a day that might well be his last, you met only small groups hastening home or to a favorite cafe. With the result that for several days when twilight came—it fell much quicker at this time of the year—the streets were almost empty, and silent but for the long-drawn stridence of the wind. A smell of brine and seaweed came from the unseen, storm-tossed sea. And in the growing darkness the almost empty town, palled in dust, swept by bitter sea-spray, and loud with the shrilling of the wind, seemed a lost island of the damned.

And here is a paragraph from chapter 45 of *Middlemarch*:

A good deal more than a year ago, before anything was known of Lydgate's skill, the judgments on it had naturally been divided, depending on a sense of likelihood, situated perhaps in the pit of the stomach or in the pineal gland, and differing in its verdicts, but not the less valuable as a guide in the total deficit of evidence. Patients who had chronic diseases or whose lives had long been worn threadbare, like old Featherstone's, had been at once inclined to try him; also, many who did not like paying their doctor's bills, thought agreeably of opening an account with a new doctor and sending for him without stint if the children's temper wanted a dose, occasions when the old practitioners were often crusty; and all persons thus inclined to employ Lydgate held it likely that he was clever. Some considered that he might do more than others "where there was liver";—at least there would be no harm in getting a few bottles of "stuff" from him, since if these proved useless it would still be possible to return to the Purifying Pills, which kept you alive, if they did not remove the yellowness. But these were people of minor importance. Good Middlemarch families were of course not going to change their doctor without reason shown; and everybody who had employed Mr. Peacock did not feel obliged to accept a new man merely in the character of his successor, objecting that he was "not likely to be equal to Peacock."

Notice that in both passages the language is dry, the style thoroughly literary. We find no funny business about "point of view" or other naturalistic devices; instead we are conscious of being held within an utterly conventional verbal procedure, language as communication. In *The Plague* we discover at the end that the narrator is Dr. Rieux, who is a person in the novel, but this seems no more than a gesture by Camus toward modern novelistic technique. He showed that he could meet the requirements of the trade while still retaining the advantage of the impersonal, authoritative, and larger-than-life narrator. In *Middlemarch* the narrator is presumably the person whose name appears on the title page, George Eliot; but although she resorts to personal intrusion occasionally, writing as a first-person narrator, this is infrequent, much more infrequent than in other well-known and much-admired novels of the period, and most of the novel is told by a withdrawn and impersonal voice. This is the mode of the work that means more than it says.

What to call novels like *The Castle* and *The Plague* has bothered critics for some time. None of the old terms—allegory, moral tale, etc.—applies, and though the more modern methods of symbolism and surrealism are analogous, they are too limited to help in defining the mode. Perhaps definition is unnecessary. Certainly it is bound to be cumbersome. But if, as I think, we may call *The Plague* a meditative lyric in prose that uses the dialectic of contrived anecdote to explore the failure of mankind in relation to death, then we may say that *Middlemarch* is a work of the same kind that explores the failure of mankind in relation to marriage. One cannot quite substitute "sex" for "marriage," because some important elements of sexuality are left out, but it comes to nearly the same thing. The fatefulness of human sexuality is what impels not only the actions described in the novel, and not only the actions of one or another gender, but the whole work considered as an expression of transcendent and unified concern. The novel is totally but unselfconsciously exemplative. It is never, as I have said already, topical.

Thus it is unlike other English novels of its time, even unlike other novels by George Eliot. What I have suggested about its intrinsic nature may outrage critics and scholars far more learned than I. But at least it accounts for my powerful response to the novel that I find tedious when regarded in any of the more traditional ways of looking at Victorian fiction. *Middlemarch* has more in common with Dostoevsky's *Notes from the Underground*, which was published six years before it, than it has with other English novels. Is there an American counterpart? Yes. *Pudd'nhead Wilson.* These three nearly contemporaneous works, so disparate in their "contents," nevertheless share a mode of imagining that has become dominant in our time. All exceed the understandings of their authors. This excess is what all writers today—even, or perhaps especially, those who call themselves Deconstructivists—work in the hope—since it can never be premeditated, and *Finnegans Wake* and *Dr. Faustus,* for instance, lack it—of suggesting. Call it the mode of accident, of portention, of half-glimpsed intimation. Call it the myth of the myth of the archetype. Call it the comedy of the greatness of failure. Whatever you call it, it should at least be noticed by those who are interested in the history of western imagination. And I would be gratified, personally, if it were noticed in George Eliot's *Middlemarch.*

DUNCAN'S DREAM

Aimai-je un rêve?
Mallarmé

In rereading Robert Duncan's poems of a decade or so ago—rereading them, I should add, for the first time since they appeared, the life of a reviewer being what it is—I am taken by surprise at the power of my own response, even though I expected it. The sense of confirmation, the degree of it, is what seizes me. I am confirmed, confirmed again, almost "over-confirmed," in my subjugation to nearly every aspect of his writing. It is a good and willing subjugation. It is a case almost of chemical, physiological reagency, although it works in the solid jointure of intellect and sense and would not occur, I think, without a mutuality of concern, of ideas by which we both are held. But the ear is fundamental to the jointure, our kinship in musical sensitivity.

Passages 36 bears a bracketed subtitle:

> THESE LINES
> COMPOSING THEMSELVES IN MY HEAD AS I AWOKE
> EARLY THIS MORNING, IT BEING STILL DARK
> December 16, 1971

I line it out this way because that's what Duncan did, I'm certain not randomly. Wordsworth and Jonson might have, and in our esthetic environment would have, done the same. Poets write poetry all the time. Most people, nonpoets, would have written "composed," not "composing," and in that, as well as in the lining, a world of difference lies. A universe. Duncan lives in the *flow* of language, meaning the flow of time, ideas, emotions, memories, sensory feelings, everything; he lives *in* the flow, not apart from it, as most poets do; and this is one reason why, when he arrests the flow, it is so effective.

The poem begins:

Let it go. Let it go.
Grief's its proper mode.
But O, How deep it's got to reach,
   How high and wide
   it's got to grow,
Before it come to sufficient grief . . .

I know but part of it and that   but distantly,
a catastrophe in another place, another time,
      the mind addresses
and would erect within itself   itself
      as Viet Nam,   itself as Bangla Desh,
itself exacting revenge and suffering revenge,
      itself the Court and before the Court
where new judges disloyal to the Spirit of the Law
      are brought. All forces conspire
            to seat them there.

Notice in the second strophe here the distinctions between a comma, a space, and a comma followed by a space. I believe even an untaught reader could sound these differing pauses properly, for Duncan's at-home-ness in language bestows on him a power to enforce his music (as in "that   but distantly, / a catastrophe": perfectly natural and perfectly beautiful, as so much in his poetry is), and to enforce it without violence. Nor is it craft, because "craft" suggests wiliness, of which I discover none in his mature work, but only the kind of spontaneous expressiveness that ensues upon complete absorption of technique. Notice further how the syntax—not simply the parallel clauses, but the phrasings within the clauses—creates a rising tension, how it lunges forward on the beats, over the beats, a wave cresting and falling against the shore. Then notice particularly the first strophe, the italicized poem that came to the poet in darkness while he was half-awake. This is the lyrical instinct in language at its very best. Impossible to analyze. One can point to the rhythmic patterns, how they recall yet make impromptu deviations from the English convention, that so honorable convention and so lovely, and also to the diction, how it combines the contemporary vocabulary, e.g., "got," which in me evokes an impeccable thrill of vulgarity, though like everyone I use it constantly in my speech, with touches of archa-

ism, as in the capitalizations and the subjunctive mood at the
end. But these are crude academical observations. They do not explain. And hence I must say again, as I have been saying, no doubt
tediously, for thirty years, that responsiveness to art is subjective,
that the finest, profoundest expressions of it are, no matter how
clear-sighted, impassioned and in a good part reverential, and
that for this we ought to be thankful.

What is the "it" in Duncan's poem? Awareness. Knowledge.
(Here, of violence and terror.) Knowledge is suspect for the poet,
always. It is not a mode of understanding, even though our "civilization" for centuries has been trying and trying and trying to
convince us that it is. The poet says: "Let it go." But on the other
hand knowing *is* a mode of being human. It is not only inescapable, it presents us with the wish to escape only at the cost of our
own unworthiness. To be human we must accept the burden of
knowledge, including its damnable usefulness. This is the tension of the poet's mode of understanding, the mode which always
undermines itself, and from it all the other tensions, and hence
the dynamisms, of poetry arise.

Later the poet says:

> Eat,
> Eat, eat this bread and be thankful
> it does not yet run with blood
>
> At the mill the wheel no longer turns;
> the fields are in ruin.
>
> Each day the planes go out over the land,
>   And revolution works within
> to bring to an end in the rage of power
>   the works and dreams
> of a governing Art. The air is darkened.
>
> Drink, drink, while there is water.
> They move to destroy the sources of feeling.

Notice the simple perfection of Duncan's compelling us to see
and hear the primary meaning beneath the common meaning of
"source" (from Latin *surgere;* in French it still means a "spring").

The poem is somewhat long, like all the *Passages,* and is full of conflict, the poet's direct attachment to myth against the world's sundering violence, with Poundian suggestions of the Consistori de Vrai Amor and how the poet has been advocate there of *mythopoios*. Then at the end:

> I do not as the years go by grow tolerant
>   of what I cannot share and what
> refuses me. There's that in me as fiercely beyond
>   the remorse that eats me   in its drive
> as Evolution is   in
>   working out the courses of what will last.
> In Truth 'tis done. At last. I'll not
>
>   repair.

It is a resolve to be in Truth, this simple eloquence: *a poet not unaware.* Taken from the moment of half-dream. Of twi-light. A tension.

"These Lines" contains much more than is indicated by my excerpts, and of course Duncan's whole work much more than that; considered as an *oeuvre*, it is extremely complex. But it is also firmly, finely integrated, as good an example as we have in English of the poetic imagination continuously evolving within the overlapping cycles of personal and social, intellectual and emotional experience. One can find loose ends and ragged patches here and there, as in anybody's lifework, and one can find also—or at least I can—places where comprehension breaks down. I am more inclined than I used to be to ascribe these latter to the poet's failing, not mine. But the success of the whole is what I emphasize, the way the poet's life has been lived on the page in remarkable candor and in even more remarkable poetic control and distancing: perhaps the most consistent, most energetic conversion of experience into art. I do not forget W.C. Williams or anyone else, but I believe the older poets had not quite Duncan's finesse of sensitivity to the meaning of *mythopoios* in poetry of the present and to the complicated intermixture of ambition and humility demanded by its expansive potentiality.

I see such need for this kind of poetry now, this understanding. More than during the atrocities of Viet Nam and Bangla Desh. Yet I do not see younger poets who recognize this, or who even try and fail in attempting it. Again and again Duncan holds out a torch in the darkness, and no one takes it from his hand. What sorrow.

CODA

I have just been listening to a record made in 1933 by Red Norvo. I had not heard it before, and I played it several times. A fine piece of work. As far as I can hear, Norvo was playing as well in 1933 as he did in '43, '53, '63. Not that he didn't learn anything in all those years; quite the contrary. But he was a talented musician, who always played up to the limit of his technique, and just a fraction beyond.

But now I can hear some of these little cats, such as inhabit the unifarcity where I teach, saying, "Man, that's like prehistoric, that's nowhere, sleepy time down south, etc., etc." Well, Jimmy Dorsey does wobble through a couple of yodelly licks in the background, I'll grant you, which is as much as we should expect from the likes of him. But there's a fine passage on guitar by Dick McDonough, some years before electronic amplification was invented, and Norvo himself, performing on a wooden xylophone, plays beautifully. The music swings; it moves. And any time the music swings and moves it is good music, I don't care where it came from, or when. Style, mode, concept, structural sophistication, these have their place, of course. But in the end authentic feeling is what counts, and spontaneous imagination.

Do not tell me that John Coltrane was intrinsically a better tenorman than Chu Berry. That doesn't make sense, rationally or empirically. I've heard them both, I've *listened* to them both, and I know.

I'll tell you something else, little cats. It's the same with poetry. Yes, from way back yonder in the Achaian hills right down to now! And with painting, for all I know. With sculpture, architecture, photography, industrial design, cabinetmaking, plumbing, farming, shining shoes . . .

MEDITATION IN
THE PRESENCE OF
"OSTRICH WALK"

Of the two cardinals the female is both bolder and more
    "beautiful." She comes
To the railing, crest raised high, snapping her eyes this way
    and that,
Uttering the little nasal ech-ech of fear and belligerence,
Then down to the lower travis, then finally to the flagstones,
    where she feeds.
Now comes the male, seeing the way is safe, and begins to
    hull seeds and feed them
To her. The mind performs its wearisome gyrationing. The
    female accepts
These token mouthfuls, but eats on her own between them.
    She is very obviously
Able to take care of herself. Although most people say
    otherwise, and say so vehemently,
The difference between Floyd Bean and Joe Sullivan is
    distinct, crucial,
And unique. I move my hand to rewind the tape and the
    cardinals
Are gone forever. *Ora pro nobis,* my good St. Chance, my
    darling.

WHAT DOES "ORGANIC" MEAN?

Chuang-tzu, the master, is said to have said: "To have an environment and not treat it as an object, is Tao." How beautiful! One smiles and sighs, and one is truly grateful, the happiest of feelings. But then difficulties begin to appear. No doubt the first part of the statement—about having an environment—is the thorniest, but let's not discuss that now; let's agree that an environment is an environment in the ordinary sense and that each of us "has" one all the time. What about the second part? If we do not treat the environment as an object, how shall we treat it? As a subject? This is the implication. But how as a subject? A subject in our own consciousness only? Or somehow a subject in itself, a subjectivity? I think the Taoist meant the latter. Our environment is intrinsically a subjectivity, perhaps a congeries of subjectivities, or at any rate we should treat it with that possibility in mind. And what is a possibility? A dream, a wish, a fiercely ardent *desiderium.* In a by no means inauthentic sense, what is desired enough, good or evil, exists. To all this I think Denise Levertov would assent.

One day in autumn we were walking through a young woods in the interior of Maine, where Denise then lived. It is upland country. We saw many old stone fences that had marked the boundaries of pastures and meadows a generation or two earlier. Now the fields were grown in popple and birch and willow. We walked on an abandoned road. I remember a number of such walks, but no longer which walk I am thinking of, nor when it was, nor who were the others with us. The leaves of the young trees were intensely yellow in the October sunlight; they shimmered in the breeze and threw shadows, faint and dappling, on the leaf-strewn ground. It was as Denise has written in her poem about the "golden glow," which has long been one of my favorites.

I was walking ahead, conversing with someone. I heard Denise exclaim something behind me, and when I turned I saw her kneeling, holding a little brown snake close to her face in order to feel its tongue flickering against her cheek. Her expression showed neither enchantment, nor wonder, nor sensual delight, nor the gratification of worldly knowledge, but some feeling perhaps at a point where all these cross one another.

The environment contains then, not an object, but a thing. Let's call it a stone. Denise would say, I think, that the stone is— not that it has or possesses, but that it is—a subjectivity. Notice that this goes further than the insistence of the Objectivists, such as Williams, Oppen, and Zukofsky, upon the inviolable identity of the stone, which the poet may subvert by symbolic imputations only at the risk of hubris. Notice that it goes further even than the Swedenborgians, who declare all things expressive of the Godhead's loving omniscience. Identity and expressiveness are not as much as subjectivity. How does one treat another subjectivity in a nonobjective way, since in some sense, as Sartre maintained, all subjectivities are the Other? How does one know another subjectivity when knowing must be ultra-verbal, as with the stone? These are supremely difficult questions. Usually they have been answered in the formulas of mysticism, but in the present context (namely, nonascetic) these seem to me wrong. Mysticism entails transcendence, which must then be defined in special terms, quite uncustomary terms, if one is to avoid the idea of the environment as the transcended, the subordinated, the objectified. Instead we should speak of art, of esthetics, the way of the spiritual imagination, for this is a transaction among equals, or at least among equivalents—poet and stone. And for me, as I think for Denise too, this is very important. It comes as close as anything can to dispelling my fear of the human species and its lust for dominion. But is art still a mode of forcing, however slight? Is the simplest, loveliest poem flawed by an unappeasable human will to intervene? I suspect it, but I don't know it—although I know that the snake may not have been consentient in its handling— and I don't even feel able to discuss it. Does anyone now?

It was a little brown snake with a pink belly. One sees them all over northern New England. Their name is always the little brown snake, which is sufficient. What I would leave with the reader is the subjectivity of that particular little brown snake, so crucial to Denise's poems, and Denise herself as she knelt, attentive, in the golden glow of the young woods.

ELEVEN MEMORANDA
ON THE CULTURE
OF JAZZ

1. The word "Dixieland" has been in popular use since ante-bellum times.[1] It derived, probably, from a ten dollar note issued by the Citizens' Bank of Louisiana, which had the French word "dix" very prominently printed on it. In 1859 came the minstrel tune "Dixieland" by D.D. Emmett, which soon was the most popular song among soldiers of the Confederacy and, after the war, a national favorite. Nobody could know the number of traveling minstrel shows that had "Dixieland" in their names, or, later, the number of jazz and dance bands. When I was young the nation, even New England, was full of "Dixieland Syncopators" and "Dixie-land Feet-Warmers." (I recall also certain outfits like the "Dixie-land Jug Blowers," rural black groups that played what might be called para-jazz or, more generally, primitive Afroamerican music, which had little direct influence on the evolution of jazz as art, i.e., they came *after* Creole and black jazz had already become a self-conscious discipline in New Orleans. I heard these groups on records, mostly Victor, at a later time.) The first generally acknowledged jazz record was "The Original Dixieland Two-Step" recorded in 1917 by the Original Dixieland Jazz Band, a group of white musicians from New Orleans who imitated (read: stole) the black music they heard around them and took it to New York; imitated it not well, one must add, but for considerable profit. The point here, however, is this: the term "Dixieland" was common, but it was geographical and cultural, not musical. I do not remember it being applied as a generic designation for a *kind* of music until 1945 or after.

Well, I wasn't everywhere. And from 1942 to late 1945 I was precisely nowhere, i.e., in the army. Maybe the term was used to signify the kind of early jazz associated with New Orleans and Chi-

cago a year or two before I heard it so used. Lu Watters, who was
one of the originators of "Dixieland" in California, was active before 1945; the Sunbeam LP reissue of 1938–40 radio broadcasts
by the Bob Crosby band (SB-216) says that the band "was known
as the 'Best Dixieland Band in the Land,'" which is certainly
edging toward a generic use of the term. On the other hand, the
Decca 78 album of the Crosby band issued at the time of the
broadcasts does not use the word "Dixieland," and the notable
Decca reissues in 1939–40 of records originally cut earlier in
the decade by famous instrumentalists from New Orleans and
Chicago were clearly labeled "New Orleans Style" and "Chicago
Style," not "Dixieland." But it isn't possible to put dates, exact
dates, on the events of cultural change. I know this much definitely: when I was young, which means in the 1930s, the years of
my adolescence, such music was called "jazz," never "Dixieland."
Jazz included all authentic Afroamerican music of that time,
whether in the style of New Orleans, of the Delta, of Kansas City
and the western sectors, or of the East Coast, whether two-beat,
four-beat, or boogie, whether of big bands, small groups, or solo-
ists, whether mostly improvised or mostly arranged. Provided it
was played with true jazz feeling, provided it showed a direct evolutionary connection with its Afroamerican roots, primarily ragtime and the blues, provided it moved on a complex and spontaneous interplay of melodic accents and the underlying rhythmic
base, provided, in other words, it "swung," a term still in use because no one has been able to come up with a better one, provided
all these things and others, it was jazz. No question. Anyone
tuned in to it could recognize it; could recognize it even in a non-
jazz context, as, for example, Bunny Berigan's solo on the recording of "Marie" by Tommy Dorsey's pop band. Musicians themselves especially recognized it. For them, the world was divided
into those who dug jazz and those who didn't. The former were
accepted; the latter—squares and straights, the "yawners" as my
friend Don Ewell called them—were rigorously and without exten-
uation rejected. Often white and black musicians played together
in private, or sometimes on recordings, long before mixed bands
were considered publicly presentable. Ferdinand Jelly Roll Morton
recorded with the New Orleans Rhythm Kings, a white band, as
early as 1922–23; Eddie Condon recorded with Thomas Fats
Waller and Louis Armstrong in 1928; Coleman Hawkins recorded
with Red McKenzie's Mound City Blue Blowers, also in 1928, etc. I
remember one night, c. 1939, when Chu Berry sat in with the

white, basically Chicago-oriented band at Nick's after he had
finished his night's stint uptown; he played forty-odd choruses of
boom-boom blues, backed by such marvelous artists as Pee Wee
Russell and George Wettling (who would never have permitted
themselves to be called artists, a word reeking of bourgeois press
agentry in those days), and everyone was delighted—that is, everyone who was with it.

But at some point in or near the mid-1940s, the antiquarian
mind appeared, namely, musicians more interested in recreating
the early modes of jazz than in extending current modes. Often
they were called revivalists, and who knows their motives? Some
were accomplished musicians who could have played anything.
One cannot doubt that their love of the free and bluesy jazz of the
1920s was genuine, or that they believed they could still contribute something, however little, from their own musical imaginations functioning both formally and emotionally within an earlier
mode; for these musicians their own least variation on "Dippermouth" or "Salty Dog" was an act of humility. But others were awful musicians, imbued with awful self-righteousness. The point is
that with the appearance of these musicians, whether they were
good, bad, or rotten, came the term "Dixieland" as the name for
the *kind* of music they played. And then for a while you could hear
real jazz in the mode of ensemble improvisation on one side of the
street, and fake jazz, or "Dixieland," on the other. In Chicago in
the late 1940s, for instance, I heard jazz, truly fine jazz with
hardly ever a cliché, played by Muggsy Spanier, Darnell Howard,
Don Ewell, Baby Dodds, Papa Yancey, Jimmy McPartland, and
scores of other older but still active musicians, and I heard Dixieland—I'll drop the quote marks now—played by Doc Evans and
the growing number of other young, white, untalented musicians
who worked with him. Elsewhere the antiquarian movement was
booming too, in California perhaps most of all, where the Yerba
Buena Jazz Band and the Firehouse Five and other such outfits
were making records taken note for note from the records of black
musicians made in the 1920s. And the antiquarian interest has
expanded continuously since then, and is still expanding. I think
there is not a medium-sized city in the country that does not have
at least one group of Dixielanders. In Syracuse, N.Y., where I live
now, we have several. Mostly these are amateur groups who play
for their own pleasure, or occasionally for small fees at bars or in
the city parks. A few have made a very good thing of antiquarianism, however. The white Dukes of Dixieland, or such individ-

ual white musicians as Al Hirt and Pete Fountain, have purveyed a hell of a lot of fake jazz in recent decades and for handsome rewards.

Sometime in the 1960s George Guesnon, a superb Creole musician who had stayed in New Orleans, said: "This year I put up my banjo and guitar, never to play them again. Al Hirt gets $8,500 a week, Pete Fountain the same, and Audio Fidelity Records [what a name! *H. C.*] gives the Dukes of Dixieland a check for $100,000, all this while the true creators of this art are playing for nickels and dimes. . . . I'll find one consolation; at least I could carve the pants off any banjo player in New Orleans when it came to playing jazz" (*Black Beauty, White Heat: A Pictorial History of Classic Jazz,* ed. Frank Driggs and Harris Lewine, 1982, p. 36). Perhaps Guesnon's personal brag, characteristic of older jazz players, is too much—a number of fine string musicians worked in New Orleans in the early days—but his complaint is right on.

Can the distinction between real and fake, between jazz and Dixieland, be easily and clearly drawn? In by far the greatest number of cases, yes. Jazz, even if played in a well-known idiom, has the power of originality, the assurance of the fully integrated musical sensibility. Dixieland is at best hokey, inept, stodgy. Listen to the drumming: it is often the giveaway. Great drummers of the past, Singleton, Webb, Dodds, Wettling, Catlett, could play authoritatively in any mode, including the two-beat mode of much early music in New Orleans; I'm sure the same can be said of great jazz drummers today. A Dixieland drummer, on the other hand, sounds like a fish dying on the bottom of a rowboat.

A borderland between jazz and Dixieland does exist, however, where distinctions can be made only subjectively. If this weren't the case, the job of jazz critics and historians would be much easier. I myself, though I have no objection to either term, "jazz" or "Dixieland," when properly defined and applied (just as I have no objection to "white-breasted nuthatch" and "red-breasted nuthatch"), continually run into difficulties with younger friends whose musical educations began in the 1950s or later. I can put a record from the 1920s by Joe Oliver or Louis Armstrong on my stereo, and their immediate response is: "Dixieland!" The same when I put on a record from a much later period by musicians who, though working in the earlier mode, are still producing jazz, not Dixieland. An example might be some of the records made in the 1970s by the World's Greatest Jazz Band, which on occasion came close to meriting its name. At the same time if I put on a

1928 record by Duke Ellington or a 1933 record of Fletcher Henderson, they say, "Ah, jazz." In the latter case they are right, but they are right for the wrong reason. For them everything played in the mode of ensemble improvisation is pro forma Dixieland, though they might accept certain recent experiments by Charles Mingus or Air or Coltrane's wonderful "Ascension." These same young people will often refer to a totally empty, academic, antiquarian imitation of Roland Kirk or Archie Shepp or Ornette Coleman as "jazz." Why? Because it "sounds like" jazz. The number of inferior imitators of post-bop jazz today is greater by far than the number of Dixielanders. And I suppose plenty of people, including some musicians, always respond to the sound of music, its general stylistic impressiveness, and not to *music* itself. (When Debussy orchestrated a tone poem, the "tone" was everything, or nearly.) When I was young, I'd say 80% of the lindy-hoppers, both black and white, danced to the sound of the Basie band and never heard the music of Buck Clayton or Lester Young.

To my mind a good deal of Dixieland was played before the word became an accepted generic term. I don't mean simply by crass vaudevillians either, people like Clyde McCoy and Sophie Tucker, for instance, or the pit bands at the Minsky burlesques. I mean Red Nichols and the various groups he put together from the late 1920s to the late 1930s, which included, I grant, many first-rate musicians, such men as Frank Teschemacher, Bud Freeman, Gene Krupa, etc. Some of my friends disagree with me about Nichols. Ok. But we can have no doubt whatever about the white genre of pre-Dixieland Dixieland that was represented by the Original Memphis Five, Sam and Lester Lanin and Guy Lombardo, Ted Lewis and Ben Bernie, the myriad slop-bands on dime-store labels, Spike Jones and other funny-bands: this genre did originate intellectually (if such inanity and corruption can be said to have contained any thought at all) somewhere near the white reaction to serious jazz, both black and white, of the period 1920–35, and it was more damaging to jazz as a significant component of American civilization—I'm certain of this—than all the socially downward snob-pressure on "brothel music," "nigger music," etc. On the other hand, a few contemporary groups that most critics would call Dixielanders in my definition of the term seem to me perhaps real jazz bands. I respond appreciatively, i.e., viscerally, to at least some of the records made by the New Black Eagle Jazz Band out of Harvard, for although much of their work is taken verbatim, so to speak, from old records, their solo breaks and width such purity of musical devotion and such sensitivity to phras-

stop-time passages as well as their ensemble choruses are done with such purity of musical devotion and such sensitivity to phrasing that I am half convinced I am hearing real jazz. Still, a large element of antiquarianism informs their work—I don't mean merely imitativeness but self-conscious archaism—and if anyone wants to call them Dixielanders—nostalgic sentimentalists—it's ok with me. Again, I am told one can still hear real jazz of the old mode in New Orleans; not in the tourist traps of the "French quarter" but in shabby clubs on the outskirts; and I have heard a few records that lead me to think this may be true. (What is even more interesting is the recent emergence of young black and white musicians, educated and creative, who are giving New Orleans a new jazz, partly traditional, partly cajun and zydeco, partly rock, partly bop and post-bop, yet more than merely an amalgam: a distinct regional music.) But the whole question of what might be called "serious" Dixieland vis-à-vis jazz is so confusing and subjective that I doubt my capacity, or anyone's, to write about it, and anyway that isn't my purpose.

My purpose is to tell my younger friends that when they hear records from the beginning of jazz down to the 1950s and beyond, made by real jazz musicians trained in the modes that came before bop, whether black or white, northern or southern, they are hearing jazz, not Dixieland, and it makes no difference whether the opening and closing choruses are played in harmonic riffs or contrapuntal improvisations. My purpose is not only to discriminate the real from the fake, but to oppose generic judgment wherever it arises, and to define "jazz" and "Dixieland" by reference to musical rather than merely formal, historical, or cultural criteria. Listen. Listen hard and long. Then perhaps someday a tentative judgment of value may be provisionally attempted.

2. Often I have heard the term "contrapuntal" used, as I have just used it, to define the mode of ensemble improvisation in the authentic jazz of New Orleans and Chicago before, say, 1940. Years ago I heard a white somebody on the radio say that such jazz is like a fugue by Bach, that it is "vertical" as well as "horizontal," and that one must listen to it in the same way that one listens to Bach. In some sense this is true; one can find a few records made by musicians so powerful, each in his own ongoing imagination, that they create simultaneous continuous independent musical statements which are nevertheless united in the collective sensibility of the group. This music is truly contrapuntal. It is also rare. In my listening to most early jazz I hear far more resemblance to the call-and-response pattern of black (and many other) folk traditions than to European counterpoint. The lead instrument, usually trumpet, plays a phrase, to which the other instruments, trombone, clarinet, rhythm, etc., give answers. These may be and usually are somewhat overlapped, fitted together in very complex movements. But one does not listen vertically, one listens sequentially. And this skipping back and forth among the instruments as they call and respond irregularly against the fundamental beat, not at all in the rhythmically fixed chordal polyphony of Bach, is what gives jazz its particularity, authenticity, and immanent cultural autonomy among all the world's musics. It is what makes the music swing.

3. Why were so many of the young Dixielanders, the revivalists in the 1950s and 1960s, fourth-rate musicians? Because they lacked spontaneity and inventiveness, what is commonly called "creativity." (Hideous word.) And why did they lack these qualities? The reasons are many. But it's worth noting that by about 1950 older musicians associated with the jazz of New Orleans and Chicago, I mean those who were still active, had become so desperately fed up with playing the same old ninety-three tunes in the standard early repertoire—can you imagine playing "Muskrat Ramble" five thousand times?—that they too had lost spontaneity and inventiveness, and had begun to play by rote, imitating themselves, working with routine segues and endings, playing hackneyed licks, etc. (This was the burden of all jazz musicians who made their livings in clubs; even Charlie Parker relied on his own long-used riffs in his later work.) I don't wish to name names among the older musicians because what I'm saying does not apply to all by any means. But young musicians who worshipped, often quite literally, these heroes of early jazz, and who attended too many ordinary nights at Nick's or Condon's, and who never heard the older musicians at their best, since recordings, especially before the advent of tape and taped live performances, seldom captured the best jazz: these young musicians willy-nilly imitated what they heard, the most tired and tiring manner of performance. Moreover certain tunes lend themselves particularly to lifeless renditions (the right word), things like "Squeeze Me" and "South Rampart Street Parade," which are favorites among the Dixielanders. One could assemble an immense library of such music, and some people have.

4. At this point a title for these expositions comes into my mind: "Memoranda on the Culture of Jazz." Nearly all the years of my life have been influenced and affected deeply by jazz; yet I have been afraid to write about it, afraid of my technical ignorance. Well, in old age my fears retreat a little. What I am writing now are the thoughts, impressions, and feelings that have occupied my mind very largely and for a very long time, the important things I remember about the culture of jazz, as distinct from the music itself; which is to say that I am writing memoranda of my life addressed to myself. I wish I could write a book, or many books, an ample and systematic account; no other topic is more important to understanding the predicaments of American civilization in the twentieth century. Such a work would be impossible for me at this point, but maybe these quick, unsystematic notes will have a little value for others as well as for myself.

5. Jazz, like poetry, is where you find it. An eclectic listener will discover more to enjoy than a listener who comes to the music with theoretical or, worse, faddish predeterminations, and in fact the eclectic listener in the long run will attain better understanding as well. My own tastes range from early to late, and go back beyond early to ragtime, minstrel tunes—"Waiting for the Robert E. Lee" still seems to me one of the greatest songs ever written, on a par with "Gee, Baby, Ain't I Good to You," "I Got It Bad and That Ain't Good," "Round Midnight," etc.—and even back to some compositions by Louis Gottschalk, which are closer to jazz than most of what we hear today as ragtime (always excepting Max Morath), and a few by Stephen Foster; not to mention thousands of other tunes in totally different musics. For that matter I still cannot wholly fathom how any musically gifted person can fail to respond to good jazz, any good jazz. The first I heard, about 1932, was by accident in a small farming community in the Litchfield Hills of Connecticut. I took to the music with an immediate fascination that has lasted fifty years or more, and I am as sure as I can be that my first response was totally musical, not cultural. It had to be. At that time I had not only never heard jazz, I had scarcely heard *of* it. The culture of jazz did not exist in the Litchfield Hills in 1932, where thought and feeling were still functionally located in the eighteenth century. Yet the culture of jazz existed elsewhere, it now exists almost everywhere, and it is very powerful; one would be an idiot to ignore it. My mother, who was probably more talented in music than I (we both had "perfect pitch"), and who had an enormous store of musical knowledge in her head, could not respond to jazz at all. I remember an evening, perhaps in 1941, when as a favor to me she joined me in listening to the weekly "prime-time" broadcast by Benny Goodman on the radio. One of the numbers was "The World Is Waiting for the Sunrise," played by a small group, Goodman himself, Mel Powell on piano, plus bass and percussion; and probably the performance, though live, was close to the record that was issued at about that same time. It was not great jazz, not quite, but it was good, and at that time it was without doubt exciting: played *molto up-tempo* but with delicacy. Goodman was still capable of a little originality and feeling in 1941, and Powell had a new piano style that many of us found extremely attractive. (I think I hear his influence in pianists as far apart as Erroll Garner, Ralph Sutton, Bud Powell [no relation], and Bill Evans, though Mel Powell left jazz after only a few years and became a "classical" composer. Goodman himself at that time was in the process of becoming a classical clarinetist.) It was, as I say, a fast and driving performance, and musically—I mean in terms of harmonic and melodic and rhythmic invention—at least interesting; to me it was more than interesting; but at the end my mother said simply: "My, I should think it would be exhausting to play like that." I can explain this only by inferring that my mother did not hear what I heard. (She had gratefully listened through many exhausting performances of Mendelssohn's violin concerto.) She did not hear the jazz as music but only as a cultural phenomenon or affect. And because she could not hear it, she could not feel it. I insist, in this case anyway, that this order of consequence, hearing before feeling, was correct. She was, of course, no less musically inept when it came to jazz than the overwhelming preponderance of other people her age, mostly white but including also a proportion of blacks that would surprise many people.

It is not enough to say that my mother was a genteel, lower-middle-class American lady whose capacities for sensuous response were repressed, or that her receptivity to black music (in this case played by whites) was closed by bigotry. Neither of these is true. I cannot prove it, but I can—and do—assert it. She just couldn't hear that music. That is to say, her musical training (she began studying violin at the age of four) was so hemmed in by European modes, from Gregorian chant to Prokofiev, that jazz was as foreign to her in its basic musical concepts as Chinese opera. It was organized noise, to the principles of which she hadn't a clue.

And I've met hundreds of other music lovers who are like her in this respect, people of all ages, my mother's generation, mine, that of my younger friends, that of the eleven-year-old presently residing in my house, who is exactly the age I was when I heard my first jazz record.

As a poet I never met another poet older than I who understood jazz as music. All my older friends—Allen Tate, Delmore Schwartz, Louise Bogan, and others—were jazz deaf. So were all other older poets about whom I knew anything at all. (Kenneth Rexroth might appear an exception, but to my mind his use of jazz in both poetry and prose was not intrinsic to his sense of himself as artist or critic, and was tinged with insincerity.) Among poets my own age I have met one or two who love and understand jazz, but none who has written intelligently about it. Most of my contemporaries have only a kind of nostalgic feeling for the "swing era." (Even Malcolm X in his autobiography, where he speaks of the jazz scene in Boston and New York during the late 1930s, the time when he himself was a champion lindy-hopper, says nothing of the music as music. For him it was, apparently, no more than a cultural adjunct.) Only when I come to poets who are ten years or more younger than I, i.e., those whose musical educations began after 1945, do I find any number, though still comparatively few, who write about jazz with understanding; and even most of these are distinctly limited in their historical perspectives. Early jazz is dismissed as funk, old-timey, down-home, etc. For some in the baby-boom generation, the beginning of jazz is the work of Charlie Parker. For most it is the work of Miles Davis, e.g., "Bitch's Brew," which one of my students once called the "anthem of my [his] generation," or possibly the work of John Coltrane; often it is mixed up with religion, eastern or Islamic, as it was taken up later by Pharoah Sanders, for instance. But ignorance remains. Very, very few of my intelligent young friends—I mean none whom I know well—are willing to sit through Shepp's "Mama Too Tight" or Blythe's "Tradition."

Two prime examples of poets who relied on music continually in their writing and who grew up poetically during the jazz age, but who were utterly jazz deaf, are Louis Zukofsky and Paul Goodman. No point in lamenting this, much as I love the work of both men; they did what they did, and did it superbly. But they both represent the kind of nonresponse to jazz by musically talented people that simply baffles me. Further, why do young people, those born after 1945 and including both blacks and whites, respond in large numbers to black rock, Motown, and even the so-called Chicago blues, but only in small numbers to Afroamerican jazz? Is it simply faddism that lets them "hear" Diana Ross and be deaf to Dinah Washington? As I say, I'm baffled.

Cultural factors *are* important in jazz, therefore, much as one wishes it were otherwise. Arthur Taylor, in his marvelous book of interviews with fellow black musicians in the period 1969–71, *Notes and Tones*, which had to be privately published in Europe in 1977, and only a good deal later, in 1982, was taken on by an American publishing firm, Perigee Books, reverts many times to the question of whether or not the word "jazz" is an appropriate name for Afroamerican music. This was at the height of the Black Power movement, the strongest moment so far of affirmative ethnic awareness among blacks, including black musicians. It was the time of what was called "freedom music," a term with both political and musical meanings. Most of those interviewed by Taylor had come out of the bop era twenty years earlier; they were fairly young, in other words, and not at all hesitant to express their ethnic feeling militantly, to say repeatedly that Afroamerican music is black music only, and that whites have no place in it—certainly not the white managers, booking agents, record producers, and other such white parasites who have fattened for years on the profits generated by black performers and composers. But the general implication was that white musicians and even listeners have no place in jazz either. As for the word "jazz," most of those interviewed disclaimed it, saying that it was a white imposition on black culture and that owing to its origin in the argot of commercial sex it always was and still is a put-down, a term of vilification. A certain truth adheres to this. Without doubt my mother's generation made a connection between jazz and brothels, honky-tonks, barrel houses, etc., whether or not this connection resulted in prejudice in particular cases. And without doubt also, such a connection did exist; it wasn't imagined. That is part of the culture of jazz, the enormous affective conglomeration that surrounds and almost buries the music. It is a function of the universal attitudinizing tendency of the human mind.

But my mother and her generation are long since dead. Art Taylor's interviews of more than a decade ago have changed nothing, and the word "jazz" is used as widely as ever, by blacks as well as whites, and has survived for eighty years or more while thousands of other words in the folk vocabulary have disappeared. For my part, I doubt that if anyone could discover the authentic etymology of the term, which is unlikely, it would reveal a white origin. I suspect its earliest form (apparently pronounced "jass," as it was sometimes spelled) emerged in black common speech, maybe from an African proto-word, and I suspect also that it pertained to a folk concept of sexuality as such, whether commercial or not. If, as most people now know, there is a noncultural association between jazz and sex, by which I mean a purely sensual association, then let us rejoice, for Pete's sake. In our time of academical solemnity, sex has gone out of the other arts. Am I wrong in thinking there is more sex in a landscape by Corot than in all the self-conscious sexual metaphors of painters and photographers in the past twenty years? Myself, I say in honest, hopeful humility to my black co-nationals: be proud of the word "jazz." It is yours. It is a survivor. It has entered every language in the world. It means just what it says.

In other words, it means a little more than "Afroamerican music." I write this latter term often, but it is awkward, it is a little too special, and when repeated it becomes tedious. "Afroamerican music" is a name. "Jazz" is a name, a description, and an explanation all in one.

A word that should be much more offensive to everyone is "blues." This does come from white usage, I expect, and probably, almost certainly, from a time long before the emergence of a clear Afroamerican identity, that is, from the time of the plantations when the "darkies" were heard moaning low down in the slave quarters, an African but not yet Afroamerican music. "Blues" is white imposition if there ever was any! And it distinctly is *not* suitable to the forms, whether eight, twelve, or sixteen bars, to which it is normally attached today. How can "Roll 'Em, Pete" or "Cherry Red" be called blues? I do not mean by this that a certain significance doesn't reside in the connection between the word and the thing, and especially in the fact that most blues are ironic or defiant rather than melancholy, though to me this significance is not enough to overcome the inaptness of the term. But there's nothing to be done. "Blues," even in its grammatical ambiguity, is a fixture of our speech.

6. The critics and historians—black and white, American and European—simply do not take account of known facts. Their leaning over backward to give blacks due credit—what has been called Crow Jim—distorts history. Examples are many and not at all hard to find if one listens to the recorded evolution of jazz with sufficient sensitivity and care. For instance, when "jazz came up the river from New Orleans," this migration was not limited to blacks alone. White musicians made the journey too, notably Paul Mares, George Brunies, Leon Rappolo, and Jack Pettis, who formed the nucleus of the New Orleans Rhythm Kings (first called the Friar's Society Orchestra), and who had as much or nearly as much influence on the development of jazz in Chicago after 1923, when most of them returned, however briefly, to New Orleans, as had Joe Oliver, Jelly Roll Morton, Louis Armstrong, or the almost legendary Freddie Keppard, who had played in Chicago as early as 1911. This can be heard on records and to a certain extent documented in the oral or written statements of young Chicagoans of that time, some of whom are living and working today. Some young people who haven't listened think the New Orleans Rhythm Kings, commonly known by its initials, NORK, must have resembled the Original Dixieland Jazz Band, ODJB; an error—the two bands were worlds apart. Yet I have never seen this mentioned by the critics. More recently, some black musicians, Dizzy Gillespie among them, have emphasized the affinity between Afroamerican music in North America and Afroamerican music in Latin America, as if that reinforced the case for black exclusivity. But they do not point out that the folk forms of Latin American music, such as the Brazilian samba, derive, both melodically and rhythmically, as much from European as from African sources. And how about the gypsies? Who can say how much flamenco influenced Django Reinhardt, except that it was a lot, or how much Reinhardt influenced all American jazz guitarists after about 1937? Certainly there was some direct connection.

How can American blacks, in the massiveness and solidity of their cultural accomplishment, be hurt at all by the truth? How can anyone?

Another point. The fact, cited so often that in spite of its truth it has become tedious, that white musicians have often stolen their material from blacks, and have profited immensely from the theft, is hardly ever balanced by critics against another obvious fact, namely, that blacks—and whites—steal material from one another. How much has Joe Williams profited from "Saw Mill Blues," which he undoubtedly first heard on a record made by an obscure singer from New Orleans named Pleasant Joe, backed by a group of musicians associated with New Orleans, Sidney Bechet, Hot

Lips Page, Sammy Price, Danny Barker, Pops Foster, and Sid Catlett, plus Mezz Mezzrow from Chicago, the recording done in 1945
on the King Jazz label? As one might expect, the version by Pleasant Joe is far better, far more expressive, than the treatment,
which is the right word exactly, given the song by Williams. Pleasant Joe is never mentioned, and the composer, Socks Wilson, is
someone of whom I know almost nothing. But how much would I
bet that he or his heirs are getting royalties? About a nickel. And
of course such thefts and profitings have occurred over and over
again, probably tens of thousands of times, in the history of jazz,
to say nothing of the other arts.

You might think that the ascription of generalized good or evil
to a particular race would have been thoroughly discredited by
now. Indeed, in obvious cases it has. But it creeps back in when
the topic at hand is complicated and not obvious. What I am trying to do here is keep my own frequently declared objection to racial bias unsullied, to the extent possible (and no one can hope to
be totally clean), by stupid criticism and warped history. To which
in justice I must, and very willingly do, add the observation that
by far the greater number of stupid critics and warped historians
are white.

7. A reason more cogent than ethnic feeling for objecting to the
word "jazz" is precisely its naming property: it categorizes the
music it refers to. Young jazzpersons now are quite clear in their
desire to admit no restrictions, to keep all their options open.
Terms like "jazz," "classical," "dodecaphonic," "European," "African," "Indonesian," or any others of like nature, including "space
music" and "acid rock," are solely critical designations, meaning
that they apply to what has already happened, not to what is happening now or will happen tomorrow. Classification is a penchant
of the academic mind, not the creative. I believe this reasoning
among young musicians is sound, important, and must be part of
every artist's awareness.

Yet we cannot talk without words, most of which are names.

I also believe it is necessary for young musicians themselves to
apply their openness of mind across the board, as, for example—
one which will seem unlikely to many of them—in recognizing
that Wild Bill Davison at his mature best was not typical but
unique: no one else in history played a cornet the way he did. No
category. In such cases one's approval or disapproval becomes
solely a matter of taste, as it should with all work by great artists.

8. But the question underlying all others in considering the culture of jazz is, obviously, the relationship between blacks and whites with respect to the music. This is what everything I have written so far in these memoranda leads up to, with the same inexorability that our lives in this society lead up to it. It cannot be evaded; it must not be evaded. But how grievously it hurts the few of us who are torn every day by the severance between the truth of art and the truth of reality, which can never be healed! As I write this my radio is tuned to the local station of the National Public Radio network; the program is one of a weekly series on Duke Ellington, his recordings, the musicians who worked with him, his beliefs and concepts, reminiscences by those who knew him— a splendid and appropriate tribute. Although most of the people heard on this program are black, a significant minority, both musicians and others, are white. Ellington himself, as far as I am aware, never held that Afroamerican music is an exclusive black prerogative; nor did most other black musicians of his generation, or even later. When Charlie Parker, who was and is one of the three or four greatest jazz heroes, once visited California and heard a young white trumpet player named Chet Baker, he returned to New York and said to Dizzy Gillespie, Miles Davis, and other black trumpet players who worked with him: "You better look out, there's a little white cat out on the Coast gonna eat you up" (*Coda*, no. 157 [Oct. 1977], Toronto, p. 6). It was the music that counted most for Parker.

And for many, many more in those days. Sidney Bechet, who was an irascible, sharp-minded man deeply embittered by the mistreatment of blacks in America, was nevertheless as happy to record with such white musicians as Muggsy Spanier and Wild Bill Davison as he was with Buck Clayton or Louis Armstrong. So he said, and I believe him. When he was in Europe, where he lived for many years and where he died, he played with white musicians most of the time, I think, and he certainly played almost entirely for white audiences. The Europeans were without racial bias—mostly. That is, partly. Comparatively. And this meant not only musicians and jazz audiences, but, which is more important, restaurateurs, hotel-keepers, and society in general. A black musician could work in France and at the same time enjoy an ordinary, comfortable, middle-class life, which has never been the case in this country, and still isn't, in spite of the power of black rebellion. Many younger black musicians, including some of those interviewed by Art Taylor, are militant and exclusionary in their attitudes toward white musicians. They have insisted that Afro-american music is theirs and theirs alone—I remember hearing an interview with a group of young black musicians, whose names I no longer recall, from CBS/Toronto in about 1971, in which the young blacks said exactly this, said it clearly, articulately, emphatically, and *without rancor;* it was an *a priori* article of their belief—and they have pretty well enforced their attitude. What has been their whole accomplishment in this, culturally and socially, is open to debate but not to proof; they have accomplished something. Granted, a fair number of black groups could be listed that have used white musicians in the past fifteen years, and vice versa. Earlier, the case of Juan Tizol in the Ellington band is practically legendary. Moreover blacks and whites have sometimes taken separate courses on solely musical grounds, exploring different ideas, then merging again, e.g., as Hannibal Peterson and Lou Soloff assimilated their different concepts of the trumpet in a new avant-garde under Gil Evans. But the larger truth is that few white musicians are now working with blacks in musically significant ways. In my own lifetime I have seen jazz changed from the one sector of American civilization in which blacks and whites could work together in spontaneous freedom, respect, and affection to a sector in which racial bias is more operative than in most others.

This is an oversimplification, of course. In any exhaustive discussion my statement about the former openness of relationships between black and white jazz musicians would need to be qualified by a reference to the spurious cultural and social advantage that blacks then felt, i.e., during the early stages of their ethnic musical development, in associating with whites. And so on. Many such qualifications will occur to every reader, and if I ask indulgence for omitting them, it is precisely because any thorough discussion would be not just exhaustive but exhausting, and could never be finished in my lifetime. The drift of what I am saying will not be impeded by a lack of sociology.

At the same time, for the sake of clarity if nothing else, one must repeat over and over again the imperative that no white person *ever* underestimate the degree of resentment and animosity felt by the black population of our society for the white population. It is the paramount social, and therefore political and cultural, force of our era. Nor should any white fail at least to know (since understanding is impossible) the reasons for such power of feeling. I don't think many who are genuinely aware of American music, art, and writing in the past forty years, including of course Afroamerican, are likely to make these mistakes. But we, the aware, know also that we are very few in proportion to the whole, and that our capacity for affecting the rot and iniquity we see everywhere around us, both far and near, is next to nothing.

Meanwhile jazz has spread throughout the world. Very good jazz is being played in every country of Europe on both sides of the curtain (even in the Soviet Union, where the Kremlin has been forced to acknowledge popular demand and is permitting public performance of jazz in the hope, certainly forlorn, of co-opting it); also in Japan; also in Australia and New Zealand; somewhat less good jazz comes from India; in Latin America one cannot always distinguish between jazz as it is known in North America and the evolution of what may be called Afroiberian music, but jazz is known and played throughout Central and South America. In fact jazz is played least well in Africa, surprising as that may seem at first to some. But jazz is Afroamerican; that is, it fuses African and European musics, it wrenches African modes to fit instruments tuned to European diatonic scales. Why should Africans themselves, who have the purity of their traditional modes all around them, even want to play jazz? (Yet some African blacks, like Dollar Brand, have contributed significantly to jazz.)

Hence, as with all matters of cultural description, the culture of jazz is complicated and confusing. It reduces itself in my mind to three questions. First, was the contribution of whites to jazz generally limited to those musicians whom we identify with "Chicago style" (including the New Orleans Rhythm Kings and many others who did not come from Chicago), beginning with Beiderbecke and Trumbauer in the mid-1920s and extending through the best periods of such younger musicians as Bunny Berigan, Pee Wee Russell, Jack Teagarden, Bobby Hackett, etc.? Secondly, did later white musicians, such as Chet Baker, Gerry Mulligan, Conte Condoli, Lee Konitz, Louis Bellson, Charlie Haden, Roswell Rudd, etc., really fail to contribute anything important to Afroamerican music? Thirdly, will jazz ultimately be damaged by too much racial inbreeding, so to speak, now that it has extended itself so far from its folk base and into the realms of self-conscious and thoroughly conceptualized, often highly technical modes (moogs, electronics), even assuming it can retain its vitality as it continues to move from clubs to concert halls and then to academic workshops? My answer in all cases is: yes.

Afroamerican music is black music. It derived from black

sources and has been developed almost entirely by black musicians. A few white musicians contributed something, but very few, though many have played fine jazz. In the work of Art Tatum I hear not only Earl Hines but Joe Sullivan. Everyone knows that Lester Young acknowledged Frankie Trumbauer as one of his models. Lee Konitz and Paul Desmond have certainly given something, however little, to the World Saxophone Quartet. And what about Miles Davis, who has influenced so many blacks, musicians and others? Listen to his work in 1945 when he was struggling to make a place for himself alongside Gillespie and Parker; then notice how his music changed when he came into contact with white musicians like Mulligan, Gil Evans, the Birth of the Cool Band, etc. It is clear, at least to me, that Davis came into his own only after he had assimilated the ideas and styles of white musicians, although his development thereafter was personal and nearly unique; that is, whatever influences Davis absorbed, his genius cannot be depreciated thereby, nor his contribution to Afroamerican music diminished. And so on. But how little the white contribution has been, and how relatively unimportant! Take the evolution of the tenor sax, which is the jazz instrument *par excellence,* though one could not have predicted this from the quality of tenor playing in 1925. Consider the line of development: Coleman Hawkins, Chu Berry, Lester Young, Ben Webster, Don Byas, Lockjaw Davis, Sonny Rollins, Dexter Gordon, John Coltrane, Roland Kirk, Albert Ayler, Archie Shepp, et al.—not one white musician among them, nor can one think of a single white tenorman, though we have had some great ones, who added anything to this main thrust. It is as if Bud Freeman and Stan Getz never existed (though I believe Lester Young did once hint that he got something from Freeman as well as from Trumbauer). Pee Wee Russell, who was to my mind one of the real giants of jazz, a white musician who should probably have been playing with Duke Ellington for years, was a lonely, isolated genius, for although many black musicians gladly praised him and worked with him, none imitated or learned from him. This is the most conspicuous and to me personally the most dismaying fact of the culture of jazz.

And much as I would like to give my attention to the art alone, the music, and leave the culture to anthropologists, I cannot do it. Jazz has been the most prominent part of my own esthetic life for more than fifty years; yet I am white, a Yankee, a countryman. I have listened to jazz, played it, written about it, and have been conscious of its influence in all my writing. But where do I stand in relationship to jazz, this black people's music? Do I stand anywhere at all?

Of course I do. I have listened, played, written, and been influenced: these are reality, the historical data that are multiplied almost incalculably in the lives of others and that must be accounted for in any theory of jazz culture, any theory whatever.

I have always believed that music is the only pure art, by which I mean the paradox of an art that in its concreteness is totally abstract. I am speaking of music in itself, ordered sound and rhythm, with all titles, lyrics, and cultural appurtenances of any and every kind stripped away. I know that certain combinations of pitch, texture, and rhythm educe from me a *frisson* that is completely physical. This is the sensual expressiveness of music, nonliterary, nonconceptual, abstract and consequently meaningless in the strict sense, and to my mind it is therefore the basic expressiveness not only of music but by analogy of all other arts as well. ("All art aspires to the condition of music," as Schopenhauer, not Pater, first remarked.) This sensational expressiveness is what accounts for my first immediate response to jazz in a time and place that limited my knowledge of the culture of jazz, Afroamerican culture, to something almost infinitesimally slight and utterly academic; no young American today could imagine it. But I have a good friend who like me is a poet, musician, and lifelong devoted listener to jazz, and who believes, as contrary to me, that the concreteness of music conveys significant, emotional, more-than-sensory meaning. It is not abstract. He believes, in fact, that a hypothetical stranger who was devoid of all cultural knowledge, but who was still a human being with a human language and normal human affective capability—such a person could listen to pure jazz, as sung or played without words, titles, or any other external references, and infer from the concrete pitches, timbres, and rhythms the essential Afroamerican experience; moreover he could put the right names on it: misery, anger, humiliation, self-mockery, despair, paranoia, all of which are literary and cultural designations. Of course we are not hypothetical strangers; it would be impossible for any person of mature judgment in this world now to isolate the art from the culture, except by means of an envisioned fantasy in a disciplined mind. We live in reality. We know that the music is black, and we know something about what being black means. Consequently neither my friend nor I (nor Leonard Bernstein) can prove his point, though I continue to believe my position is the more reasonable (and the more helpful in any investigation of esthetic expressiveness in general). But my friend and I are both white, and though we disagree about how it works, we know that jazz does function esthetically, emotionally, and intellectually in our lives with as great an intensity as it does in any black person's. We have suffered too, we have been drunk and crazy, we have loved and despaired. And we have listened.

9. Well, we do not *know* these things. (I keep hauling myself back to strictness.) We cannot "cognize," in Schopenhauer's sense, and we certainly cannot "intuit" the quality of any black person's feeling about jazz. But one thing we can and do know is the extent to which black culture has infused all American culture in our lifetimes: yes, in spite of bad relationships between the races, and more particularly the exploitative relationship of whites to blacks. I am speaking here not simply of high culture, by which I mean jazz plus the literature, painting, cinematography, etc., of all black artists, but of the common culture. I do not know any way to quantify the part of my students' vocabularies that derives from black speech, for instance, but it is large, large enough to be considered determinative. It is large in my own speech, and was large almost fifty years ago when I was in high school, i.e., after my family had moved from rural New England in the 1920s to metropolitan New York in the 1930s. In those days we were hep, as later generations were hip, though neither spelling captures black pronunciation. In our walking we trucked, with a little knee-and-toe bounce, and in our dress we were zooty and wore porkpies on our heads. We knew the finger code that signified whether one was prowling for sex, muggles (marijuana), or coke/horse. We had that basic black beat, that sensuality, that joyous and pained physicality, going constantly like the tsp-tsp-tsp of a ride cymbal in our ears, our viscera, far stronger than the cadences of Marlowe or Milton or Robin Burns (though in some of us a fusion occurred, a transpiration). And what else in American culture of the twentieth century has been any good?

I don't mean that white folk culture wasn't important. In any living society no element of folk consciousness can be unimportant. I trace aspects of my own feeling to the Okies, the underworld of Chicago, white crapshooters and pool-hall aficionados, and especially to American Jews, whose trenchant metaphysical optimism in the face of absurdity has been continuous in my conscious and subconscious awareness since I first encountered it

(not long after I encountered jazz). But none of these by themselves, nor all together, nor even all that they represent, could
have saved us from the final breakup of puritanism that con-
vulsed America before and during the First World War. The writing of Hemingway and Sinclair Lewis helped; so did the music
of Stravinsky and Copland; Charlie Chaplin and Buster Keaton
helped a lot; but they could not have done the trick by themselves.
It took a massive pervasion of black sensuality to do it.

From my back window, where I'm working now, I just saw a
black schoolgirl, about fourteen or fifteen, walking up the drive to
the apartment complex where she lives across the way. Every two
or three steps she paused, swayed right or left, moved her feet,
moved her hips and shoulders, and then went on. Maybe she was
practicing a dance step, but I don't think so. The way she held her
head seemed to indicate that she was far away, thinking of something else altogether. How common a sight this is. We white people
have seen it—usually without real comprehension, without real
seeing—for 150 years and more. I take it that this is the pure African presence in our midst. We assume this unconsciously, since
it is so self-manifest. White civilization could never have created
jazz, and that act of creation, together with the racial experience
behind it, belongs to blacks.

Take dancing, it having emerged here unforeseen. I was raised
to dance reels, square dances, quadrilles, with an occasional
waltz or fox-trot. (Fox-trot: how quaint. Yet graphic too. I wonder
if it also emerged from far distant black speech? The dictionary
doesn't help me.) When I abruptly encountered the eagle rock,
etc., pecking, trucking, lindy-hopping, etc., I was shocked by
such public abandon, as it seemed, into not dancing at all. To this
day I can't do it, and I regret my loss, although probably in any
case I'd have been more interested in the music than the dancing.
Think how dance music has evolved, as distinct from jazz: swing,
rock, twist, hustle, disco, rap, etc. All derived from blacks. It is
simply impossible to conceive American culture without the massive, almost absolute predominance of black sensibility.

Whenever I see a white kid moving the way that black schoolgirl
did, I have a spasm of hope.

But for the moment let's leave matters of sensibility and imagination, and speak solely of the Negro voice. I use the term "Negro"
technically, as it would be used by ethnographers, to mean people
descended from the negroid inhabitants of Africa between the Sa-
hara and the Congo. Why, then, have we never had a first-rate

white jazz singer? (Jolson, that whore.) Maybe a few have come close enough to let us feel they might have made it if they had been really interested: Connie Boswell, Mildred Bailey, Helen O'Connell, Kay Starr, Janis Joplin, Bonnie Raitt, etc. Occasionally we hear someone we think had everything it takes, e.g., Wingy Manone if he had not been so determined to imitate Armstrong. But the fact is that the voice of the blues is a black voice (and the blues are integral to jazz). Don't ask me to define it. I leave that to the bio-ethno-linguists or whatever they call themselves. But I hear in the *typical* black voice—singing, speaking, or the marvelous intonations that are neither—a doubling or distancing effect that I do not hear elsewhere, the vocable or sonant foundation with a shadowy "other voice" in front of it. It is not mere huskiness. I'm told that in operatic terms it is called "veiling." Whatever it is, it is the voice of the blues, and apparently a genuine racial trait, a part of black physical being. And where would America be without it? I can scarcely imagine. I know that I cannot sing the blues with my voice, but I have tried many times to do it on paper—I mean in all kinds of writing—and I believe in a few instances I have succeeded. What is more important, I see and hear it in the writing of many other white authors who I know have no sensitivity whatever to black music as such. The voice is permeative. It is distinct, very distinct, but not disjunctive. When Marian Anderson sang Shakespeare's "Fear no more the heat o' the sun," it was among the great songs of all the world. I resist saying "blues," lest I smudge the genre, but in a larger sense it was a blues.

Need I give more instances? I can't make a catalogue, though what a sweet job it would be. *Huckleberry Finn, Porgy and Bess, The Emperor Jones, Carmen Jones,* and fully half or more of our theater, film, and literature today, I mean works engendered primarily by *serious* white artists and producers (though collaboration gradually becomes more possible), Faulkner, Farrell, Barber, O'Keefe, Steinbeck, T. Williams, and so on and so on—even such a WASP as Joyce Carol Oates reveals a demonstrable black influence—these are not jazz, far from it, but they are imbued with honest (if only because unconscious) semijazz feeling. And what would our life be like without it? A damn sight shallower than it is, though some say it is shallow to the point of drying up anyway. But wherever I go, from the interior of Maine to the interior of Los Angeles, I find people talking, walking, thinking, feeling in ways directly and obviously traceable to black culture. And this is good. This is our vitality and our compassion, the two qualities without which we could never stand a chance of resisting the rhythmless, computerized force of military capitalism that oppresses us.

10. No catalogues. But at least let me quote from Charles Mingus, always worth hearing. This is from his autobiography where he is quoting himself in an interview with an English journalist (*Beneath the Underdog*, Penguin edition, p. 252).

> If you're talking about technique, musicianship, I guess the British can be as good as anybody else. But what do they need to play jazz for? It's the American Negro's tradition, it's his music. White people don't have a right to play it, it's colored folk music. When I was learning bass with Rheinschagen he was teaching me to play classical music. He said I was close but I'd never really get it. So I took Paul Robeson and Marian Anderson records to my next lesson and asked him if he thought *those* artists had got it. He said they were *Negroes trying* to sing music that was foreign to them. Solid, so white society has its own traditions, let 'em leave ours to us. You had your Shakespeare and Marx and Freud and Einstein and Jesus Christ and Guy Lombardo but we came up with *jazz*, don't forget it, and all the pop music in the world today is from that primary cause. British cats listen to our records and copy them, why don't they develop something of their own? White cats take our music and make more money out of it than we ever did or do now! My friend Max Roach has been voted best drummer in many polls but he's offered less than half of what Buddy Rich gets to play the same places—what kind of schitt [*sic*] is that? The commercial people are so busy selling what's hot commercially they're choking to death the goose that's laid all them golden eggs. They killed Lester and Bird and Fats Navarro and they'll kill more, probably me. I'll never make money and I'll always suffer 'cause I shoot off my mouth about agents and crooks and that's all I feel like saying tonight!

A pretty fair nightful. Mingus is exaggerating a little in this passage, but very little, and he is not exaggerating his own depth and intensity of feeling one bit; in fact this speech is tame. But Mingus did nevertheless respect some white jazzmen, and elsewhere in his book he speaks several times of his dream of a "colorless" jazz community.

11. Of course, if my words about the fusion of cultures are taken literally, they are wrong. And how else should they be taken? The severance again: I am rent between word and thing. Listen to Roy Eldridge speaking of the years when he, a black, was a star performer with the white bands of Gene Krupa and Artie Shaw, back in the 1940s: "Man, when you're on the stage you're great, but as soon as you come off, you're nothing. It's not worth the glory, not worth the money, not worth anything" (Leonard Feather, "Jazz in American Society," *The Encyclopedia of Jazz*, 1960, pp. 82–83). We can and usually do read such words glibly because in effect we have read them thousands of times before: the humiliation of the black artist unable to eat, lodge, travel, or even walk down the street with his—or her (ask Lena Horne)—white colleagues. Can we understand that, can we feel it—the wrench and crack-up? No. But when Eldridge says that such experiences are not worth anything, he means *anything*. And he quit, and went to live and work in Europe, like scores and hundreds of other black American musicians from the 1920s onward. Some, like Eldridge, stayed a short time; others stayed for years, for the rest of their lives. Can we understand that, feel the extent of suffering which could force such difficult and sorrowful decisions? Never.

Yet they went to Europe, that is, to the seat not only of the music which they opposed to their own but of the social attitudes and economic systems which they knew had defiled them, deracinated them. Is that significant? When Melvin B. Tolson, the great American black poet, decided to get out, he went to Liberia. Was it *only* that jazz musicians could make better livings in Paris and Stockholm than they could in Lagos or Dar es Salaam? I am sure these questions point to something of extreme importance in black experience, though I know I cannot define it and that any attempt to do so would end in confusion. We who are white in North America, no matter how we may have been isolated, alienated, and afflicted by personal and social disease, can never know what it is to be black in North America, the precise pain, the dimension of that pain—and the comedy of it too, for to laugh, however wryly, however "blackly," is to survive. And blacks, unlike most whites now, are survivors.

Today in our smugness or fear—or both—we like to think that the black predicament has eased. This is a profound mistake. We see popular black artists, entertainers, and politicians moving freely in white vicinities where they would have been excluded fifteen or twenty years ago. But can we know what such people experienced *before* they became popular? No. Can we intuit the extent and depth of feeling they have for their fellow blacks who are not popular, who will never be popular, who are living in poverty and subjugation? No. Though this is something I can only infer, I am certain of it: no white in North America can feel for other whites anything like what a sensitive black feels for other blacks. And the importance of this is so huge and ramified that I can only dimly perceive it.

We are faced with a solidity, the barrier between black and white, which is as if made of glass—vision from both directions penetrates it, but not much else.

Except the music. Somehow we must account for the genuine response of a considerable number of white people to black music. This is a solidity too, a fact, as has been recognized by many observers. Twenty-five years ago Billy Taylor, the fine black pianist, wrote: ". . . jazz is no longer the exclusive medium of expression of the Negro. As the Negro has become more articulate and outspoken, his music has reflected his growth. And in each stage of its development, jazz has become more and more the medium of expression of all types of Americans and, to a surprising degree, musicians from other lands and other cultures" (Feather, p. 85). What Taylor seems to be saying is that as jazz becomes more sophisticated, which inevitably (like all art) it does, it moves closer to other sophisticated musics. This is undeniable. The debt of black musicians twenty years ago to Stravinsky and Bartók is clear. When I was young, fifty years ago, educated jazz musicians listened to Mozart. Today they listen to John Cage or Adrian Stockhausen.

They listen also to the music of the gamelan, to calypso, to the stridencies of the *barrio*, to anything at all that pleases them. Their roots may be Afroamerican, but their searchings are international.

People have said since time began that in order to understand the "other" a person must in some sense be the "other." In a separate essay ("Got Those Forever Inadequate Blues") I have gone even further; I have said that the blues and the part of jazz deriving from the blues are musically, concretely, functionally the best expression of existentialist feeling in the twentieth century, i.e., that all of us who are aware of the human predicament in the post-Nietzschean world are black. Billy Taylor was writing before Black Power and freedom music, but these, even in their historical necessity, do not change what he wrote. On the basis of everything and anything I know about artistic evolution in all times and places, Taylor was right. He still is. Much as we wish to grant the historical justice of the Afroamerican claim to exclusivity in Afroamerican music, on the larger ground of culture we cannot do it. It is willy-nilly impossible. Just as we cannot imagine a good music that does not have its roots in locality, neither can we imagine a good music that is not sensually apprehensible by people in general. We would laugh at anyone who maintained that a pianist from Leipzig could possess, by virtue of that alone, a better understanding of Bach than a pianist from Ottawa. When it comes to Bach, we are all Teutons. When it comes to jazz, we are all black. Or, as Mingus said, we are colorless.

Just recently I heard a group put together by Hank O'Neal: Al Cohn, Benny Carter, George Duvivier, Don McKenna, and Jake Hanna. No black or white. Just great music.

Beyond this, one dreams. I don't know what a poet's dreams are worth—maybe not much. But I dream continually of a great session where race, or more properly speaking ethnicity, has no significance at all, where "culture" is irrelevant, where every performer and listener participates freely and equally in the bodily and spiritually wrenching, exhilarating, purging experience of jazz-in-itself. I dream the dream that I thought was an actuality when I was a boy. It cannot happen. But may we not go in that direction?

NOTE

1. A number of friends have helped me in this writing, and I owe them thanks: David Budbill, George Dennison, John Engels, Mitchell Goodman, Bradford Morrow, Hank O'Neal, and Paul Zimmer.